THE CATHOLIC UNIVERSITY OF AMERICA
CANON LAW STUDIES
No. 200

Force and Fear in Relation to Delictual Imputability and Penal Responsibility

AN HISTORICAL SYNOPSIS AND COMMENTARY

A DISSERTATION

Submitted to the Faculty of Canon Law of the Catholic University of America in Partial Fulfillment of the Requirements for the Degree of Doctor of Canon Law

by

ALAN EDWARD McCOY, O.F.M., J.C.L.
Priest of the Franciscan Province of Saint Barbara

THE CATHOLIC UNIVERSITY OF AMERICA PRESS
WASHINGTON, D. C.
1944

Nihil Obstat:

Juniperus Doolin, O.F.M.,

Patricius Roddy, O.F.M., S.T.D.,

Censores Deputati

Imprimi Potest:

Gregorius Wooler, O.F.M.,

Minister Provincialis

Oaklandae, Calif., die XX martii, 1944

Nihil Obstat:

Ludovicus Motry, S.T.D., J.C.D.,

Censor Deputatus

Imprimatur:

+ Joannes J. Cantwell, D.D.,

Archiepiscopus Angelorum

In Civitate Angelorum, Calif., die XV maii, 1944

Printed by

The Schauer Printing Studio, Inc.

Santa Barbara, Calif.

TO

ST. BERNARDINE OF SIENA

ON THE

FIFTH CENTENARY OF HIS DEATH

1444-1944

TABLE OF CONTENTS

PART II

CANONICAL COMMENTARY

CHAPTER III

CHAPTER IV

Foreword

The following study deals with force and fear as factors excusing from crimes and from the punishments due to them. To secure a complete view of this question it is necessary to trace the historical development of the terms and concepts involved, and, upon this consideration of the gradual unfolding of the canonical doctrine in the works of the earlier authors, to study the present status of the question as determined by the Code of Canon Law.

In the historical synopsis the influence of Roman Law concepts will be noted, as well as the introduction of its precise terminology into canonical doctrine. But the present work will not go into detail in regard to the Roman Criminal Law aspects of force and fear, for although the terms used by the early canonists and even by modern authors in these matters came from Roman Law, they were taken from the Roman Law on contracts, and not directly from Roman Criminal Law.

To delineate the beginnings of a systematic and complete treatment of force and fear precisely as excuses from crime and punishment it will be necessary to dwell at some length on the doctrine of the decretists and decretalists in regard to force and fear in the field of contracts and in connection with oaths. For it is in these discussions that the fundamental notions regarding these causes as excuses in penal matters first developed. The present canonical doctrine on these factors in criminal matters came largely through the great Scholastics of the 13th century, who in turn drew from the teaching of Aristotle (B.C. 384-322) in these matters. And so it is to these Schoolmen—Alexander of Hales (ca. 1170-1245), St. Bonaventure (1221-1274), St. Thomas of Aquin (1226-1274), John Duns Scotus (1266-1308)—that one must look for the real beginnings of a systematic and logical treatment of this subject.

The second part of this dissertation will consider the teaching of the present Code of Canon Law on force and fear in regard both to the imputability of the action committed under such duress and also in regard to the penalty determined for such an action. These norms are to a great extent identical with the doctrine of the pre-Code canonists, which had developed gradually through the years following the great Schoolmen. However, the few changes made by the Code will have to be discussed together with their relation to the pre-Code doctrine.

The one purpose throughout will be to provide a clear view of the wise norms of the Church in these matters, and thereby to furnish a definite set of rules that can easily be applied to the individual case of a materially criminal action committed under the stress of force or fear. It is hoped that these pages will evince to at least some extent the factual foundation for the term '*Mater Ecclesia*' even when one speaks of the Church in regard to penal matters. Surely even in this, the fulfillment of her solemn duty to protect the social order committed to her care, the Church is solicitous not only that the Justice of God may be shown forth, but also that His Mercy become evident to all.

The writer wishes to extend a sincere expression of gratitude to his former Provincial, the Very Rev. Martin Knauff, O.F.M., of happy memory, and to his present Provincial, the Very Rev. Gregory Wooler, O.F.M., for the opportunity of graduate study in Canon Law. Profound appreciation and gratitude are due also to the members of the Faculty of the School of Canon Law of the Catholic University for their cordial and generous assistance, and to all others who have helped in the preparation of this work.

PART I

HISTORICAL SYNOPSIS

As in so many problems of Canon Law, the treatment of force and fear in the law of the Church depends to some extent upon Roman Law for its origin. As will be noted in a later chapter, the very definitions of force and fear as introduced into Canon Law, and still in use among canonists, were borrowed from Roman Law sources. However, there is a peculiar note in regard to Roman Law as a foundation for canonical discussions on force and fear in penal matters.

Roman Law, at least during the imperial period, undoubtedly admitted causes such as ignorance, necessity and grave fear as diminishing or totally excluding imputability for a criminal action.[1] The principle was quite clear with regard to grave fear. Although grave fear did not exclude all freedom of action on the part of the will and hence did not entirely excuse from guilt or the consequent punishment, it did lessen the guilt and in proportion to this excused from the punishment to some extent.[2] Yet this penal doctrine of Roman Law did not have any considerable direct influence on Canon Law. It was rather the Roman Law doctrine on contracts which first influenced canonists in this matter. For it was from the canonical discussions on force and fear as exempting from the obligation of fulfilling various contracts or promises that the canonists came to treat directly of the problem of excuse in penal matters.

The greatest impetus to a logical and systematic treatment of this subject came from the moralists of the fourteenth and later centuries, who followed the great Scholastics in their philosophical approach to this legal question. And the present-day canonical doctrine on force and fear in matters of delictual imputability and

[1] Cf. Ferrini, *Diritto Penale Romano, Teorie Generali* (Milano, 1899), pp. 130-144, 206-207.

[2] D. (40,12) (16,1) ; D. (27,6) (7,1). Cf. Ferrini, *Diritto Penale Romano*, pp. 206-207.

penal responsibility stems directly from this source rather than from the Roman Law doctrine on the subject.

Questions regarding force and fear in criminal actions were touched upon by some of the early Fathers, notably by St. Ambrose (ca. 340-397), by St. John Chrysostom (ca. 344-407), by St. Augustine (354-430), by St. Gregory the Great (ca. 540-604), and later by St. Isidore (ca. 560-636). But these are usually found in isolated remarks on individual problems and do not provide matter for a lengthy consideration on the subject.

The *Decretum Gratiani* (ca. 1140) by collecting the various opinions of the Fathers and of the Popes on this subject gave an impetus to a more detailed consideration of the effect of force and fear on various human acts. And so it is logical to start the historical synopsis with the *Decretum* of Gratian. The Roman Law material and the earlier references in the patristic or papal documents will be noted as they enter the canonical discussions either through the *Decretum* or later decretals or directly from the Roman Law sources.

CHAPTER I

FROM GRATIAN TO THE COUNCIL OF TRENT

The *Decretum Gratiani* occasioned many important doctrinal developments in the sphere of ecclesiastical penal law. Although in the *Decretum* there is found little which gives a definite foundation for a complete theory of imputability and responsibility regarding forced acts, the canonical doctrine on moral imputability in general gradually developed during the four centuries from the time of the *Decretum* to the Council of Trent, that is, from about the middle of the 12th century until the middle of the 16th century.

A review of this period is of value and interest in the present study inasmuch as during this time the notions of force and fear were clearly outlined. But it must be stressed that throughout this period the canonical discussions on force, and especially those on fear, centered mainly around the problem of excuse from the obligation of contracts and of oaths. A common disregard for a complete, logical consideration of fear as an excuse in criminal actions will be noted up to the very end of the period. Although the beginning of certain fundamental doctrines as expressed in present-day legislation may be noted herein, it remained for later canonists to draw upon the findings of moral theology to give a complete picture of the entire problem together with the solutions.

ARTICLE 1. GRATIAN AND THE DECRETISTS[3]

In the *Decretum Gratiani* and in the decretals the question of the legal implications of forced acts is treated in various places. It is seen in connection with the validity of resignation, of baptism,

[3] This period is treated very thoroughly by Kuttner, *Kanonistische Schuldlehre von Gratian bis auf die Dekretalen Gregors IX*, Studi e Testi, n. 64 (Città del Vaticano: Biblioteca Apostolica Vaticana, 1935), II, c. 2. "*Nötigungsstand*", pp. 299-333. The present article relies to a great extent upon Dr. Kuttner's research in the doctrine of this period. Hereafter this work will be cited as: Kuttner, *Schuldlehre*.

of ordination by heretics, of monastic vows, of marriages, etc.[4] But the question of the imputability of criminal acts committed by one under stress of force or fear is treated in a much less satisfactory manner. And it is this last question that is of particular concern in an historical conspectus of this problem of force and fear in regard to the imputability of delicts and the responsibility for penalties.

Among the canons introduced by Gratian very few give definite bases for the development of a theory of imputability regarding forced acts. Foremost among these canons is that of the Synod of Ancyra (314), which excused from guilt *(veluti extra delictum constituti)* those priests who, during the persecution of Diocletian and Maximian, were dragged to the pagan altars and forced to sacrifice.[5] Gratian also produced numerous authorities from the Fathers to show that a woman who suffered rape through violence did not lose her *pudicitia.*[6] *Coactio* was mentioned also in regard to other cases, but no detailed treatment of its kinds and degrees was given.[7] In questions regarding the binding power of a forced oath and the consequent imputability of the breaking of such an oath there is a richer field of material for investigation in regard

[4] St. Augustine (+430), c.22, C.XXII, q. 4; Innocent I (402-417), c.111, C. I, q.1; Nicholas I (858-867), c.2, C. XV, q.6; Felix III (483-492), c.118, *de cons.,* D. 4; Alexander III (1159-1181), c.19, *Comp.* I, *de cons. et matr.,* IV, 1; c.2, *Comp.* II, *h.t.,* IV, 1 (cc. 14, 15, X, *h.t.,* IV, 1); Innocent III (1198-1216), c.1, *Comp.* III, 34 (c.3, X, *h.t.,* III, 42), and practically the whole title *"De his quae vi metusve causa fiunt".* (X, I, 40).

[5] C. 32, D. L. Cf. also the letter of Pope Nicholas I (858-867) to Emperor Michael (842-867), written in 865: c.7, D. XXI; Jaffé, *Regesta Pontificum Romanorum ab condita Ecclesia ad annum post Christum natum MCXCVIII* (editionem secundam correctam et auctam auspiciis Gulielmi Wattenback curaverunt S. Loewenfeld, F. Kaltenbrunner, P. Ewald, 2 vols. in 1, Lipsiae, 1885-1888), n. 2796. Hereafter this work will be cited as JK, JE, JL.

[6] These are contained in C. XXXII, q. 5; cc. 1, 2 (St. Ambrose [+397]); 3-7, 9, 12 (St. Augustine [+430]); 8 (St. Isidore [+636]); 10 (St. John Chrysostom [+407]); 6 (§§ 2, 3), 11 (St. Jerome [+420]); 13 (St. Gregory the Great [+604]).

[7] Innocent I to Bishops and Deacons of Macedonia (414): c. 111, C. I, q. 1; JK, n. 303 (heretical ordination); Felix III to Bishops of Sicily (488): c. 118, *de cons.,* D. IV; JK, n. 488 (rebaptism).

to imputability. This problem however was treated separately in all canonical treatises of that time, and this arrangement is now used also by Kuttner.[8]

It can easily be seen that the real problem of imputability was not touched in the canons which dealt with the priests who were forced to offer sacrifice, or with the woman who was forced to submit to an assault. For in neither case was there any question of an act of the will on the part of the one who was forced.[9] The consideration of whether or not guilt was removed or in any way lessened by such a state of compulsion is what led to lengthy canonical discussions regarding the kinds and degrees of force.

I. The General Teaching

1. The Canonical Distinctions

Rufinus (+ca. 1190) took the lead in establishing the first series of distinctions. He based his distinctions on the one notion of *coactio* as embracing the various kinds of force. Strangely enough, he first distinguished *coactio* according to degrees rather than according to species. Thus he differentiated *coactio modica* and *coactio violenta.*[10] He then further subdivided *violenta coactio* into *absoluta (passiva)* and *conditionalis (activa).*[11] Rufinus' teaching on this point dominated the theory of the older decretists down to the time of Huguccio (+1210). It then gave way to the allied notions derived from Roman Law as contained in the pretorial edict

[8] *Schuldlehre,* pp. 314-333.

[9] This is seen especially in the references to rape: St. Augustine (c. 3, C. XXXII, q. 5): " . . . Sed cum pudicitia sit virtus animi, . . . nullus autem . . . in potestate habet quid de sua carne fiat, sed tantum quod annuat mente vel renuat . . ."; Rolandus, *Stroma ex Decretorum Corpore Captum,* ad C. XXXII, q. 5. This work is cited from Kuttner, *Schuldlehre,* pp. 299-333. Hereafter it will be cited as: Rolandus.

[10] Rufinus *(Summa Decretorum,* c. 1, C. XXII, q. 5 [ed. Singer, Paderborn, 1902] p. 400): " . . . sciendum est ergo, quod coactio duplex est, modica, scil. et violenta . . . " This work will be cited as: Rufinus.

[11] Rufinus *(loc. cit.)*: " . . . violenta alia absoluta, alia conditonalis, vel aliis nominibus passiva et activa".

quod vi metusve causa, which found its way into Decretal Law at the time of Alexander III.[12]

A. Coactio Modica

According to Rufinus *coactio modica* was that force or compulsion which did not contain an attack of any great strength *(quae maioris fortitudinis impetu caret).* The threat of arson was most frequently given as an example of this.[13] However, from the definition one sees that cases of vincible physical force likewise had to be included here. Sicardus (+ 1215) is the only one of the older decretists who admitted that such force offered some excuse for the actions committed under its influence.[14] He declared that the *modica coactio* should at least imply a mitigation of the punishment, even though it could not offer a full excuse. He took as his standard of comparison, the power of resistance of the *vir constans* and defined as *modica* that force *"quae non caderet in virum constantem."* He borrowed this concept from the notions of Roman Law.

B. Coactio Violenta

A *coactio violenta* was defined simply as the opposite of a *coactio modica,* and the decretists divided it into absolute and conditional, also termed passive and active.[15]

[12] Alexander III (1159-1181) to the Bishop of Worcester: c. 2, X, *de his quae vi metusve causa fiunt,* I, 40 *(Comp.* I, c. 2, *h.t.,* I, 31); JL, n. 14131.

[13] Rufinus *(loc. cit.):* " . . . modica est, quae maioris fortitudinis impetu caret, ut cum quis, nisi ei iuretur, domum cras incendere minetur . . . " Huguccio *(Summa Decretorum,* ad c. 1, C. XXII, q. 5): " . . . modica est, que maioris fortitudinis impetu caret, ut cum quis alicui suadet vel adulatur vel minatur incendere domum vel aliud leve, ne hoc vel illud faciat." This work is cited from Kuttner, *Schuldlehre,* pp. 299-333. Hereafter it will be cited as: Huguccio.

[14] Sicardus *(Summa Decretorum,* ad c. 1, C. XXII, q. 5): " . . . modica de dampno pecunie vel periculo persone, que non caderet in virum constantem, hoc imputatur . . . ; non excusat, tamen alleviat." This work is cited from Kuttner, Schuldlehre, pp. 299-333. Hereafter it will be cited as: Sicardus.

[15] Rufinus *loc. cit.; Summa Coloniensis* (ad. c. 1, C. XXII, q. 5): " . . . violenta, que atrocitatem facti continet, violenta quoque alia est absoluta,

Thus we have for the first time the various species of force clearly defined by the canonists. These categories are sufficiently wide to make possible a classification of the different types of force exerted upon the will of another.[16]

1. *Coactio absoluta* or *passiva* consisted in a complete domination of the one forced, in so far as his body was brought to do something against which his will rebelled completely.[17] As the canonists pointed out, in such a case there was no real *agere,* but only a *pati,* because the idea of activity, which presupposes some act of the will, was essentially excluded.[18] Hence there was no basis for imputability.[19] However, the decretists introduced the question of the *culpa praecedens,* the case wherein a person occasioned such circumstances through his own fault.[20] Kuttner points out that this was really an artificial or substitute guilt *(ein Schuldsurrogat, eine Scheinschuld,*[21] for the decretists included here every type of guilt involved in a case through which one encountered these circumstances (that is, had fallen into the power of another). But real guilt was present only when the *culpa praecedens* existed as the true and efficient cause of such a state of affairs, and not merely as an objective, mediate cause. Many canonists did not consider

sive passiva . . . [aliam] conditionalem dicimus . . . " This work is cited from Kuttner, Schuldlehre, pp. 299-333. Sicardus *(loc. cit.)*: " . . . violenta alia passiva vel absoluta, alia activa vel conditionalis . . . " For other references cf. Kuttner, *Schuldlehre,* p. 302, note 5.

[16] Kuttner remarks that it is to the credit of the canonists of this period to have established these logical categories on which was based the terminology of the later Common Law and also the present day law *(vis absoluta* and *compulsiva).—Schudlehre,* p. 303.

[17] Rufinus *(loc. cit.)*: " . . . violenta et absoluta est sive passiva, que est per attractionem, ut id fiat, cui coactus nulla ratione consentiat, ut si alicuius manus super aram ydolorum ad turificandum violenter poneretur."

[18] Rufinus *(loc. cit.)*: " . . . et sciendum quoniam qui absoluta coactione urgetur, non facere, sed pati potius dicitur."

[19] Rufinus *(loc. cit.)*: " . . . quod autem fit violenta et absoluta coactione numquam imputatur . . . "; Huguccio *(loc. cit.)*: " . . . hec ex toto excusat . . ."

[20] Rufinus *(loc. cit.)*: " . . . (nunquam imputatur)nisi quis suo delicto in huius coactionis angustias venerit, et hoc similitudine illius, quem sua culpa traxit ad insaniam, qui si hominem furens occiderit, restituta sanitate poenitentiam pro homicidio subibit."

[21] *Schuldlehre,* p. 304.

this latter fact and imputed guilt whenever any *culpa praecedens* was involved. However, some did oppose this doctrine.[22]

2. *Coactio Conditionalis.* This type of force (also called *activa)* was so named because the aggressor gave his victim a choice between a present or a future evil on the one hand and compliance with his demand on the other. So the condition for escaping the evil was the choice of complying with the demand of the aggressor. Thus there was listed the example of a person holding a sword at the throat of another and threatening to kill him immediately if he did not comply with the wishes of the aggressor.[23] Now if the victim complied, he really acted voluntarily, and although he was under threat, he called his will into play.

The problem naturally arose regarding the relation between guilt and a forced act of the will. In other words, was a diminution or exclusion of guilt to be postulated only when the force was, beyond the point of a moderately strong constraint, a *coactio violenta,* a complete *maioris fortitudinis impetus,* or also when it simply implied a *metus "qui caderet in virum constantem?"* Rufinus and his followers passed over this question when treating of the general problem and were satisfied with the conclusion that the victim really placed an act of his own will. In a word, his action connoted more of the element of *agere* than of *pati.*[24]

There are repeated references to the axiom of Roman Law, *"Coacta voluntas est voluntas."*[25] The acceptance of this axiom

[22] *Summa Lipsiensis* (ad. c. 1, C. XXII, q. 5): " . . . quidam tamen dicunt, quod sive culpa sua in[s]ciderit in illam sive non, non debet ei imputari, potius enim pati intelligitur quam agere. violenta itaque coactio et absoluta semper excusat secundum eos, modica nunquam." This work is cited from Kuttner, *Schuldlehre,* pp. 299-333.

[23] Rufinus (ad. c. 1, C. XXII, q. 5): " . . . conditionalis vel activa est, que habet fieri aliqua conditione periculosa presentis vel futuri facti instanter proposita ut si aliquis iratus gutturi tuo gladium poneret dicens: 'nisi iuraveris, continuo morte morieris'."

[24] Rufinus *(loc. cit.)*: " . . . qui autem secunda (conditionali) coactione impellitur, metum quidem patitur, sed et facit aliquid, ne quod metuit patiatur." *Summa Coloniensis (loc. cit.)*: " . . . qui secundum conditionalem coactionem impellitur, agit quidem, sed metum patitur."

[25] D. (4.2) (21, 5); (21.2) 22. *Glossa Codicis L.G. ad* c. 1, C. XV. q. 1, "arg. quod coacta voluntas voluntas est, ut ff. de ritu nupt. Si a patre . . .

was corroborated by St. Augustine's dictum *"Non sunt peccata nolentium, nisi nescientium."* which Augustine explained by showing that one who perjured himself through fear really wished to do so in order to preserve his life.[26] The earlier decretists stopped with this conclusion. Huguccio (+1210), however, reduced this conclusion to its logical consequences when he taught that a *coactio conditionalis* never excused, but at most mitigated the punishment.[27]

Practically, then, this rigorous view represented the opinion of the older decretists. Evidently it did not reach beyond the question of the responsible action of the will. Hence it did not consider the real problem of compulsion. This is seen in the interpretation of the canon of Ancyra,[28] which dealt with the case of priests who were forced to offer sacrifice. This canon mentioned only the *coactio absoluta* and correspondingly declared that one who acted under such force was not to be subjected to punishment.[29] In the first part of this canon was mentioned the case of priests and deacons who had offered sacrifice to idols, but for certain reasons, following their subsequent retention of the faith, were not deposed, but only excluded from the exercise of their office. Joannes Faventinus and those following him interpreted this as a case of *coactio conditionalis;* but the text gives no real basis for such a view.[30] Yet even this interpretation showed that they considered *coactio conditionalis* capable only of mitigating the guilt.

(23, 2, 22)." This work is cited from Kuttner, *Schuldlehre,* pp. 299-333. Huguccio *(ad h.c. ad v. vult ergo facere)*: "arg. quod voluntas coacta voluntas est, nam per coactionem venit quis ad voluntatem et efficitur voluntarius . . ." Cf. also Joannes Teutonicus (+1245), *Glossa Ordinaria ad* c. 1, C. XV, q. 1 *ad v. utique vult.*

[26] C. 1, C. XV, q. 1.

[27] Huguccio *(ad* c. 118 *de cons.,* D. 4 : " . . . hec in malis non excusat, ut hic, cum nullo metu et nullo modo sit malum faciendum; . . . set nec illa C. XV, q. VI, cap. I et II contradicunt, locuntur enim similiter sicut et hic de conditionali coactione. illi enim, de quibus dicitur in illis cao., non excusantur a peccato set a graviori pena, sicut ibi plenius distinctum est . . . "

[28] C. 32, D. L.

[29] C. 32, D. L, §§ 2, 5.

[30] Joannes Faventinus *(Glossa ad Decretum, ad* c. 32, D. L.): " . . . presbiteri, cum ydolis immolabant, aut violenter attracti hoc faciunt vel non; qui non attracti hoc faciunt, aut aliquo timore concussi hoc faciunt, puta

2. *Distinctions Taken from Roman Law*

A decretal of Alexander III which commanded the reinstatement of a cleric in his benefice, which the latter had renounced due to threats, mentioned for the first time in Canon Law *vis* and *metus* as designations of the kinds of *coactio*. Alexander explained his decision by the statement: *"quia quae metu et vi fiunt, debent in irritum revocari"* [31] and related it to the edict of the Roman pretor which, as Ulpian reported, originally had read: *"Quod vi metusve causa gestum erit, ratum non habebo,"* but which later indeed made mention only of the *metus,* under which *a fortiori* the *vis* was included.[32] The *Compilatio Prima* of Bernard of Pavia (+1213) brought together for the first time, under the title *"De his quae vi metusve causa fiunt,"* a group of decretals concerning this matter of compulsion. This title was taken from title 20 of the Second Book of the Code of Justinian, substituting *fiunt* for *gesta sunt.* This arrangement was carried over into the later collection of the decretals.

In place of the older canonical distinctions, there were now the Roman Law concepts: *"Vis est maioris rei impetus, cui resisti non potest,"* [33] and *"Metus est periculi causa mentis trepidatio."* [34] Therewith disappeared the older canonical arrangement in which the division according to degrees *(violenta-modica)* preceded the division according to species *(absoluta-conditionalis).* Kuttner points out that only in Bernard of Pavia is there to be found an

timore penarum vel amissione rerum, et huiusmodi, aut spontanei. item illi qui timore, aliquando penitentes revertebantur . . . " This work is cited from Kuttner, *Schuldlehre,* pp. 299-333. Hereafter it will be cited as: Joannes Faventinus. Cf. also *Summa Coloniensis* ad c. 32, D. L; Joannes Teutonicus, *Glossa Ordinaria, v. immolaverunt:* "coacti conditionaliter."

[31] C. 2, Comp. I, *de his quae vi metusve causa fiunt,* I, 31-c. 2, X, *h.t.,* I, 40, written between 1159 and 1161, addressed to the Bishop of Worcester,—JL, n. 14131.

[32] D. (4.2) 1.

[33] Bernardus Papiensis, *Summa ad Compilationem Primam, h.t.,* (I, 30); *Summa Bambergensis, ad* c. 32, D. L. These works are cited from Kuttner, *Schuldlehre,* pp. 299-333. Cf. D. (4.2) 2 (Paulus: Definition of *vis maior).*

[34] Bernardus Papiensis, *op. cit., loc. cit.* Cf. D. (4.2) 1 *(Ulpian).*

echo, as it were, of this older scheme.[35] Bernard named and defined *vis* and *metus,* then combined them again under the term of *coactio,* and finally divided this into *coactio violenta* and *coactio modica.* But these latter two notions he in turn defined according to the Roman terminology, as in fact Sicardus (+1215) had done within the older canonical scheme.[36] It should be noted that the terms *coactio absoluta* and *coactio conditionalis* were used interchangeably for *vis* and *metus* respectively by Joannes Teutonicus (+1245), Bernardus Parmiensis (+1266) and St. Raymond of Penyafort (+1275).[37]

A decretal of Innocent III (1198-1216), which he issued before the year 1200, shows no essentially new categories were thus introduced by the notions *vis* and *metus.* In this decretal Innocent distinguished the imputability of one's act in dealing with an excommunicated person *per coactionem attractus,* and of one's act *per metum inductus.*[38] Innocent declared that since in the case of the one compelled through *coactio* (as it is here called instead of *vis)* there is had only a *pati* and not an *agere,* such a one is free from punishment. Thus he gave the same reason as that adduced by the older canonists in the case of *coactio absoluta.* The glossators Laurentius (+ after 1212) and Tancred (+1235) both stated in this connection that such an *attractus* is to be compared to a

[35] *Schuldlehre,* p. 309.

[36] Bernardus Papiensis *(Summa Decretalium* [ed. Laspeyres, Ratisbonae 1860], *de his quae vi metusve causa fiunt,* I, 30): " 'vis est—non potest' 'metus—trepidatio'. quia vero in talibus intercedit coactio, videamus, que coactio excuset. coactio alia violenta alia modica; violenta est que cadit in constantem . . . modica vero est que non cadit in constantem."

[37] Cf. Joannes Teutonicus, *Glossa Ordinaria ad* c. 10, C. XV, q. 1 and c. 3, C. III, q. 1. Bernardus Parmiensis, *Glossa Ordinaria* ad c. 5, X, *de his quae vi metusve causa fiunt,* I, 40. Sancti Raymundi De Penyafort, *Summa iuris canonici* (Veronae, 1744), *De impedimento violentiae sive metus,* Lib. IV, Tit. IV, p. 505.

[38] Innocent III to the Archbishop of Nidaros (the modern Trondheim) Norway (1201)—c. 5, X, *De his quae vi metusve causa fiunt,* I, 40 *(Comp.* III, c. 2, *h.t.,* I, 23)—Potthast, *Regesta Pontificum Romanorum inde ab anno post Christum natum MCXCVIII ad annum MCCCIV* (2 vols., Berolini, 1874-1875), n. 1128. Hereafter this work will be cited as Potthast.

sleeping person.[39] Regarding the one forced through fear *(per metum inductus)*, Innocent adopted the strict interpretation that the guilt of a mortally sinful act was indeed attenuated by the circumstances of fear, but nevertheless not negated.[40] Kuttner remarks that this doctrine of Innocent is apparently traceable to the influence of his teacher Huguccio (+1210).[41]

THE DEGREES OF *Metus*

The distinction made according to the divers degrees of *metus* became of importance in canonical teaching at this time. Even before the Romanizing influence of Alexander III we meet, in individual decretists, the distinction between *metus qui caderet in virum constantem,*[42] and the *metus qui non caderet in virum constantem.*[43] But after Alexander's decretal this became the common distinction among both the decretists and the decretalists. At first this was used as an interpretation of the canonical concepts of *violenta* and *modica;*[44] later however it is seen in place of these concepts. Again the degree of *metus* which could affect a constant man wrought an excusing effect. Another term for this was *metus iustus,* also taken from Roman sources[45] and its opposite, which never excused was called *metus iniustus* or *metus vanus.*[46]

[39] Tancred *(Glossa Ordinaria ad Compilationem Tertiam, ad* c. 2, *h.t., v. coactionem)*: "absolutam; ut 50 di presb. (c. 32): nam talis comparatur dormienti . . . "

[40] " . . . In secundo vero, licet metus attenuat culpam, quia tamen non eam prorsus excludit, cum pro nullo metu debeat quis mortale peccatum incurrere . . . "—c. 5, X, *de his quae vi metusve causa fiunt,* 1, 40—Potthast, n. 1128.

[41] *Schuldlehre,* p. 309.

[42] Taken from the Digest (4.2) 6.

[43] Simon of Bisignano (+ after 1179), *Glossa ad Decretum, ad* c. 1, C. XV, q. 6): " . . . quod tamen legibus videtur esse contrarium, que distinguunt inter metum, qui in constantem, et metum qui in meticulosum potuit cadere." This work is cited from Kuttner, *Schuldlehre,* pp. 299-333.

[44] E.g., Bernardus Papiensis as quoted above, p. 14.

[45] Cf. Ulpian, D. (4.2) (7.1).

[46] Cf. Celsus, D. (42.1) (13.1); also Gaius, D. (4.2) 6. Kuttner lists the decretists and decretalists who followed this Roman distinction. *Schuldlehre,* p. 310, note 3.

Bernard of Pavia wanted to explain the objective norm of the *vir constans* through a subjective norm, namely in the light of the fortitude or timidity of the one concerned *in concreto.*[47] But the other decretists passed over this suggestion, as well as over the subtle question of Vincentius (+ ca. 1240) as to whether the norm should be *vir constans* or (as implied in the sources) *constantissimus.*[48] They rather concentrated on the objective consideration of the abstract standard. They asked: Which fear must a *vir constans* oppose, and to which fear may he be permitted to succumb without responsibility? The canonists again followed the lead of the Roman sources here. At first not only the doctrine of the canonists[49] but also a decretal of Innocent III (authentically) postulated here the threat of death or of bodily torments as alone excusing the *vir constans.*[50] But the canonists were not content to limit the excusing effect to these two kinds of *metus.* It was further asserted that the threat of taking away goods should be considered as excusing for the *vir constans.* Bernard stated this in regard to things necessary for life,[51] while Alan (+ probably after 1238) even allowed a *damnum grave* to suffice, and said the decision as to whether a damage should be considered grave would have to rest

[47] Bernardus Papiensis *(Summa Decretalium, de his quae vi metusve causa fiunt*—[I, 30]: " . . . hanc (que cadit in constantem) etiam sepe ex ipsius qui patitur magnanimitate vel pusillanimitate metimur, quia in magnanimo levis, in meticuloso violenta invenitur."

[48] Gaius, D. (4.2) 6. Vincentius, *Glossa ad Compilationem Tertiam, ad* c. 1, *de his que vi, v. constantem*: "alibi dicitur constantissimum." This work is cited from Kuttner, *Schuldlehre,* pp. 299-333.

[49] Cf., e.g., Joannes Teutonicus (+1245) *(Glossa Ordinaria ad* c. 1, C. XV, q. 6): " . . . si queris, qualis metus debeat cadere in constantem virum, dico quod talis, qui continet metum mortis vel cruciatum corporis . . . " Bernardus Papiensis *(loc. cit.)*: " . . . que cadit in constantem, sc. que continet metum mortis vel cruciatum corporis . . . "

[50] Innocent III to the Bishops of Marseille and Agde (1190)—c. 6, X, *de his quae vi metusve causa fiunt,* I, 40 *(Comp. III,* c. 3, *h.t.,* I, 23)—Potthast, n. 733; Cf. C. (2.20) 4 and 7; C. (2.4) 13.

[51] Bernardus Papiensis *(loc. cit.)*: " . . . utrum ablatio rerum inducat violentam coactionem? . . . ad quod dicimus, quod ablatio est alia illarum rerum sine quibus hec vita duci non potest, alia illarum sine quibus hec vita duci potest; prima inducit violentam coactionem . . . alia vero minime."

in the judgment of a good man *(arbitrium boni viri)*.[52] Besides this they added as excusing a *vir constans* fear rising from other sources as mentioned in Roman Law; fear of enslavement, of imprisonment, of *stuprum*.[53] These various kinds of fear they recounted in the following verse: [54]

Excusare metus hos posse puta, quia nescis:
Stupri, sive status, verberis atque necis.

Hence fear of such things was considered to affect a *vir constans* to the extent of excusing him, and his reaction was the final standard of judgment. But they did not admit such fears as excusing in case there was a *culpa praecedens*.[55]

However, it must be stressed that all these Roman distinctions, even though they always contained a question of excuse from responsibility, did not by any means refer primarily to criminal legal problems, but treated rather the question of the validity of legal actions (resignations, vows etc.) as well as protection against extorted legal claims. This is first of all clear from the selection of the fundamental Roman sources. It is obvious in them that the question entirely concerns cases of civil law, in which the pretor aims at helping the one who acted compelled by fear and grants in his behalf actions, objections, restitutions. Analogously to the

[52] Alanus *(Glossa ad Compilationem Primam, ad* c. 2, *h.t.)*: "Nota metum dampni rerum excusare . . . iste metus ita demum excusat, si valde grave dampnum timeatur, secus si modicum. set si grave dici debeat, hic arbitrio boni viri taxatur." (taken from Tancred *ad loc. cit.* with the sign "ala"). This reference is found in Kuttner, *Schuldlehre,* p. 312, note 2.

[53] D. (4.2) 4; 7; 8; 22; 23. Tancred *(Glossa Ordinaria ad Compilationem Primam, h.t.)* "Iste metus excusat et metus servitutis et metus stupri et metus verberum . . . " Damasus *(Additiones ad Glossa Ordinaria Tancredi ad Compilationem Primam, loc. cit.)*: " . . . item metus stupri, item metus subversionis status . . . item metus ablationis rerum . . . " This work is cited from Kuttner, *Schuldlehre,* pp. 299-333.

[54] Vincentius *(Glossa ad Compilationem Primam, ad* c. 2, *h.t.)*: " . . . hec omnia comprehendere potes duobus versiculis: excusare . . . " This work is cited from Kuttner, *Schuldlehre,* pp. 299-333. Tancred, *Glossa Ordinaria ad Compilationem Primam, ad* c. 2, *h.t.*; *Glossa Ordinaria ad Compilationem Secundam, ad* c. 1, *h.t.*

[55] Richardus (+1237) *Glossa ad Compilationem Primam, ad* c. 2, *h.t., ad v. coactus)*: "nisi culpa sua incidat in metum . . . "

defense against civil claims, therefore, the decretalists speak of excuse from responsibility which to them has primarily the meaning of actions, exceptions, restitutions, and not that of the removal of criminal guilt. So it can be seen that there is no conflict between these distinctions and the decision given in the sanctioned and strict teaching of Innocent III [56] mentioned above,[57] according to which "*pro nullo metu debeat quis mortale peccatum incurrere.*" But, as Kuttner argues, [58] insofar as the distinction between *metus qui caderet in constantem virum* and *metus vanus* is understood according to criminal law, the *excusare* should be applied in aid of not only the one deprived of his rights through compulsion, but also of a forced delinquent acting under similar compulsion. This analogy can, of course, apply only to criminal actions which are not mortal sins; for the case of mortal sins is governed by the strict theory of guilt, which admits the state of compulsion only as a mitigating circumstance as long as the victum of fear still placed his act with human responsibility.

II. RESULTS OF A FORCED OATH

Two pertinent questions were raised by the canonists of this period regarding forced oaths. First, what was to be said of the obligatory validity of a forced oath? And secondly, what of the imputability of its non-fulfillment? The starting point of this discussion is the decision of St. Augustine as reported by Gratian.[59] A certain Hubaldus, due to threats of death, had sworn to take his concubine as his wife, and also to drive his mother and brothers out of his house and to refuse to give them any support. St. Augustine in his decision said that the forced marriage should be held as valid, but that the rest of the oath should not be kept, since its content was illicit and since an oath should never establish or sustain a *vinculum iniquitatis.* Regarding the guilt of Hubaldus who had been forced to this oath, St. Augustine gave the rather complicated reply that whatever had been illicitly extorted should not

[56] C. 2, *Comp.* III, *h.t.*
[57] p. 11.
[58] *Schuldlehre,* p. 314.
[59] C. 22, C. XXII, q. 4.

redound as a reproach to the forced will. *(Nec enim ullo modo ad opprobrium coactae voluntatis trahitur, quod illicita conditio necessitatis extorsit.*[60]

Actually this decision was based rather on the doctrine concerning the *iuramentum illicitum* than on a consideration of the fact of compulsion. The contract of marriage being licit, the oath bound in this respect; but since it was illicit to drive out one's family, the oath could be broken in this respect. The last sentence, however, has caused some discussion in regard to imputability,—namely whether opprobrium should accrue to the forced one because of the forced oath. This could mean either that the presence of *coactio* excluded the opprobrium of the illicit taking of an oath, for such an illicit oath was in itself a sin, or it could imply the exclusion of the opprobrium which would have resulted from the non-fulfilling of the oath. If it means the latter, the question arises as to why the force is not considered independently of the lawfulness of the content of the oath, since the non-fulfilling of an illicit oath entails no opprobrium even when no *coactio* is in question. These considerations gave rise to a detailed treatment of the state of compulsion in connection with an oath. By this decision of St. Augustine the canonists were led to solve the problems of *coactio* by considering the content of the oath.

Here should also be mentioned three penitential canons, reported by Gratian, which provided a mitigation of penance for the one who perjured himself in consequence of the force he suffered. These can also be applied to assertory oaths.[61]

It is evident that the only type of *coactio* which could come into question in regard to oaths was the *coactio conditionalis,* since the *coactio absoluta (vis)* necessarily referred only to an exterior force which of itself could not compel one to take an oath.[62] Ru-

[60] This formula is repeated in the Letter of Leo I to Nicetas, Bishop of Aquileia, March 21, 458.—C. 1, C. XXXIV, q. 1 and 2—JK, n. 536.

[61] Cc. 1-3 *(poenit. Theodor.),* C. XXII, q. 5.

[62] Rufinus *(Summa Decretorum, ad* c. 1, C. XXII, q. 5, p. 400): " . . . cum ergo de coactione absoluta vel modica agitur, de coactitiis iuramentis supervacue queritur, quandoquidem et absoluta coactione iuramentum nunquam prestetur, et modica, si prestitum fuerit, semper imputetur."

finus (+1190) sketched a highly complicated scheme of distinctions in the case of an oath taken as a result of a *coactio conditionalis.* But, as Kuttner points out,[63] in all these distinctions of Rufinus and his followers it was not the *coactio* but the content of the oath that decided the question. In considering the instances in which the breaking of a forced oath was considered free from *reatus* one finds always some mention of accidental reasons or grounds, such as objective impossibility, illicitness, or finally damage for the one taking the oath, for Rufinus held that a forced oath possible of fulfiillment was not binding if it could not be fulfilled "*sine enormi damno*".[64] But he also adverted to the concept of the *culpa praecedens,* as a result of which, when the oath-content was morally possible of fulfillment, there was no excuse for the one who took the oath if he encountered these circumstances through his own fault.[65]

Such a complicated scheme was really not to the point in the consideration of *coactio.* It is self-understood that an *impossibile naturâ* did not have to be fulfilled, even though it was knowingly promised. There was also no need of the presence of a *coactio* to exclude the fulfilling of an oath which was illicit. Rufinus' distinction with reference to a *culpa praecedens* and a *damnum grave* when the oath-content was morally possible of fulfillment, was not accepted by later canonists. Rather the strict opinion was adopted. It made the licitness or illicitness of the oath-content the only deciding factor.

A decretal of Alexander III (1159-1181) furnished the foundation for this strict trend.[66] The Pope here decided that an oath even extorted *gravissimo metu* could lawfully be broken only if the fulfilling of it would lead to loss of the soul's salvation *(vergat in interitum salutis),* an expression which the decretal does not explain more fully. In all other cases it would not be without danger to break an oath *(non est tutum, quemlibet contra iuramentum*

[63] Schuldlehre, p. 319.

[64] *op. cit., loc. cit.*

[65] *op. cit., loc. cit.*

[66] C. 4, *Comp.* I, *de iureiurando,* II, 17—c. 8, X, *h.t.,* II, 24 (addressed to the Archbishop of Sens in France)—JL, n. 12293.

suum venire). The Pope did not want to advise anyone to such a step lest perjury result. But the Pope could absolve expressly in individual cases from the binding character of the oath. [67] In such a case, however, the non-fulfillment no longer involved a problem regarding the contested question of guilt.

Simon of Bisignano (+ after 1179) was the first among the decretists who referred to this decretal. He declared that the breaking of every forced oath *quod non vergat ad deteriorem exitum* was perjury. The *Summa Lipsiensis* (ca. 1186) and Sicardus (+1215) both cited the decision of Alexander III in support of the strict opinion as opposed to that of Rufinus (+1190). Numerous glosses of the decretists and decretalists followed the same principle.[68] Huguccio (+1210) who had formulated the strictest principle in regard to the general teaching on force,[69] here again urged the strictest interpretation. According to him, a *coactio conditionalis (metus)* never excluded the guilt involved in the taking of an illicit oath, since the will still acted under its own direction in such

[67] This was instanced already in the letter of Nicholas II to the Bishops of Gaul (written between 1059 and 1061)—c. 2, C. XV, q. 6—JL, n. 4447; also in a letter of Gregory VII (1078)—c. 2, X, *de iureiurando,* II, 24 (Comp. I, c. 9, h.t., II, 17)—JL, nn. 3880, 3881.

[68] Simon of Bisignano *(Glossa ad Decretum, ad* c. 22, C. XXII, q. 4): " . . . unde generaliter dicimus, quod si quis licet coactus aliquid iuraverit se facturum, quod observari ad deteriorem exitum non vergat, est observandum." *Summa Lipsiensis (ad* c. 1, C. XXII, q. 5): " . . . si sit medium quod promissum est hic, si iurans sua culpa incidit in necessitatem, implere cogitur . . . si autem sine culpa sua hoc factum fuerit, secundum quosdam ad id tenetur, quod iuravit, ut infra extra 'Sicut sancta' (c. 4, *Comp.* I, *de iureiurando,* II, 17), secundum alios non tenetur . . . secundum Jo (annem Faventinum) si non possit implere nisi cum dampno enormi, non cogitur adimplere, alioquin minime." The two above mentioned works are cited from Kuttner, *Schuldlehre,* pp. 299-333. Sicardus *(ad* C. XXII, q. 5): " . . . qui promittit possibilia et licita, si culpa sua devenit ad hanc coactionem, adimplere cogatur ut Obaldus; vel si non adimpleverit, a periurio non excusabitur, si culpa non precessit, aiunt quidam esse absolvendum, . . . alii solvere cogendum ut in vaganti (!) 'Sicut'. tertii equitate gaudentes, quod si servare non potest sine enormi dampno, quo urgatur ad inopiam, absolvatur minime: semper tamen absolutionem impetret, ne contempnere videatur." For other references, cf. Kuttner *Schuldlehre,* p. 320, note 3.

[69] Cf. *supra,* p. 9.

an instance, nor did it offer an excuse for the non-fulfilling of a licit oath, whether or not a *culpa praecedens* was involved, and regardless of whether the *coactio* was slight or violent.[70] Kuttner notes that the *Summa Bambergensis* (ca. 1210) stated this principle in the fashion of Roman Law: "*Generaliter novimus turpes obligationes nullius esse momenti*".[71] This principle implies that no one could effectively obligate himself to commit any act of moral depravity *(turpe)*, but a person could obligate himself under circumstances which were morally reprehensible *(turpiter)*, for example, when he acted under compulsion or constraint.[72]

This strict theory indeed agreed with the content of the old Augustinian decision, but there still remained unsolved the question which was raised by the phrase found in that decision—that for a forced will no opprobrium or reproach could result from an act placed under compulsion. The solution of this question demanded a consideration of the *coactio* in itself. In consideration of this the canonists crystalized a doctrine which limited the strictness of the theory. They made a separation between sin and *crimen*, between the *forum Dei* and the *forum ecclesiae*. Before God alone the strict norm or standard had its full force and efficacy inasmuch as the guilt of sin remained in spite of the *coactio*. But according to the human norm, *in iudicio ecclesiae*, the *coactio* had to be accorded a favorable consideration. Thus he who swore under duress did not draw infamy upon himself (either for the pronouncement of an illicit oath or for the breaking of a licit one).[73]

[70] *Ad.* c. 3, C. XXII, q. 5. Cf. also Joannes Teutonicus (+1245), *Glossa Ordinaria ad* c. 2, C. XV, q. 6.

[71] D. (45.1) 26 (Ulpian).

[72] Kuttner, *Schuldlehre*, p. 322, note 1; *Summa Bambergensis ad* c. 1, D. XIII.

[73] Huguccio (+1210) *(ad* c. 22, C. XXII, q. 4 *v. opprobrium)*: "i.e. infamiam; non dicitur 'peccatum'; peccavit quidem mortaliter . . . hic enim non de peccati, set de infamie opprobrio intellegitur, quod non propter hoc efficitur quis infamis"; *(ad v. stabile)*; " . . . haberet exceptionem 'quod metus causa' quoad hominem, non tamen quoad Deum. . . . set michi videtur, quod exceptio metus causa non tenet quoad Deum, etsi absolvet secundum legem fori, non tamen secundum legem poli absolvit, quia corpus, set animam absolvere non potest." Joannes Teutonicus (+1245) *(Glossa Ordinaria ad* c. 22, C. XXII, q. 4): "'ad opprobrium,' i.e. ad infamiam. non dicit ad peccatum, quia revera peccavit, quando iuravit . . . "

Infamy, then, was a symbol of *crimen* in opposition to sin. A very severe ecclesiastical penalty was not incurred if there was no infamy involved. Hence with such a distinction, the severity of the former teaching was maintained in the *forum conscientiae,* so that Huguccio could write: "There is no exception *quod metus causa* before God." But in legal practice the *coactio* was thereby recognized as an independent factor through which there was excluded any punishment decreed solely for the *crimen.* Alan (+ probably after 1238) taught the following distinction: according to the secular as well as the ecclesiastical *ius fori,* compulsory oaths do not bind, and their violation brings no infamy, but the *ius poli* imputes the crime in such a case (i.e. with the limitations prescribed by Alan). The decretal of Alexander III could be reconciled with this distinction in view of the expressions the Pope employed when treating of the obligation of the licit oath (" . . . *non est tutum quemlibet contra iuramentum suum venire"; "nec . . . dare materiam volumus veniendi contra iuramentum . . . ".)* Thus the Pope did not absolutely command that the oath be observed.[74]

Other decretalists also made use of this distinction when they wanted to depart from the strict opinion in an individual case.[75] This limiting of the judgment of the guilt to a sin before God found a certain confirmation in a decretal of Celestine III (1191-1198), who decided that one should not just say to the unwilling victims

[74] Alanus *(Glossa ad Compilationem Primam, ad c. 4, de iureiurando)* " . . . dici potest, quod super re licita metu prestitum iuramentum est obligatorium, et mortaliter peccat, qui quod iuravit non adimplet . . . set magis placet, quod metu extortum iuramentum non obliget iure fori, unde . . . qui iuravit quod solveret, potest exceptionem opponere 'quod metus causa' iure fori et ecclesiastici et secularis. nec per talis iuramenti fractionem infamiam incurrit . . . set an iure poli hoc possit? distingue: . . . peccavit tamen mortaliter iurando contra conscientiam. et hanc distinctionem hic innuit Alexander nolens precise indulgere et indistincte . . . similiter noluit precise prohibere . . ." The distinction Alan makes here is the following: "aut tunc, cum iuravit, adimplere voluit et tunc quoad Deum fuit per sacramentum obligatus, aut tunc adimplere noluit, et sic non est obligatus quoad Deum, peccavit tamen mortaliter iurando contra conscientiam; et hanc dist. hic innuit Alexander . . . "

[75] Cf. Kuttner, *Schuldlehre,* p. 325, note 1.

of a forced oath that they could break it. But on the other hand, these should not be punished *tamquam pro mortali crimine.*[76]

But not all of the canonists were content with this mitigation of the strict theory in practice. Many decretalists looked also to the content of the oath in order to determine whether its non-fulfillment remained free of guilt. They alleged that an oath could be broken without any concomitant guilt of sin not only when its observance would bring ruin to the soul, but also when the observance of the oath would endanger the welfare of the body. However, in the latter supposition the harm had to impend directly. Alan permitted the distinction between *directe* and *oblique* in this instance to be made in accordance with the judgment current among upright men *(arbitrium boni viri),* a norm very often appealed to by him.[77]

This surely approached Rufinus' norm concerning the guiltlessness of a violation of an oath in the case of an impending *grave damnum.* But the canonists after him were further concerned with whether the victim had the intention of fulfilling it at the time he took it, or whether, merely to free himself of compulsion, he had sworn the oath without any intention of fulfilling it. In

[76] "Ceterum ut agatur consultius et ab eis [iuramentum invite praebentibus] auferatur materia deirandi [perierandi?], non eis ita expresse dicatur, ut iuramenta non servent, sed, si non ea attenderint, non ob hoc sunt tamquam pro mortali crimine puniendi."—c. 6, *Comp. II, de iureiurando,* II, 16—c. 15, X, *h.t.* (According to Friedberg this reply was addressed to the Bishop of Brindisi. Jaffé-Loewenfeld [2. ed.] list it as addressed to the Archbishop of Nidaros (Trondheim) Norway, between the years 1191-1198-JL, n. 17639.) We find a certain mitigation even in Huguccio *(ad* c. 3, C. XXII, q. 5) : " . . . forte excusatur ab atroci peccato et graviori pena, quoad ecclesiam, quia minus punitur ab ecclesia—et forte a Deo—quam si non fuisset coactus."

[77] Alanus *(ad* c. 4, *Comp. I, de iureiurando, ad v. interitum):* " . . . vergit tamen in detrimentum salutis corporalis et ideo sacramentum non est obligatorium"; *ad v. salutis:* "Idem si temporalis salutis . . . hoc dico, si directe vergat in interitum, quoniam si occasionaliter, nichilominus sacramentum est tenendum, ut si quis ultramontanus iuret se moraturum Rome in augusto, set utrum directe vel oblique vergat ad interium, ad arbitrium boni viri referatur."; Bernardus Papiensis (+1266) *(Casus ad Compilationem Primam, ad.* c. 4, *de iureiurando, ad v. salutis aeternae):* "Credo quod idem esset, si vergeret in interitum salutis corporalis, nam et propter salutem

the first case the oath was binding; not so in the second. But even in the latter case the mere taking of the oath sufficed to coonstitute a sin. Alan applied this distinction also when judgment was to be rendered according to the *ius poli;* Damasus (+ after 1216) used the same distinction quite generally, as did Joannes Teutonicus (+1215) (at least in his *Apparatus* to the *Compilatio Tertia),* and above all Tancred (+1235).[78]

But Tancred's doctrine in general differed from the common doctrine as based on the decretal of Alexander III. He inclined to the doctrine of the decretist Bazianus (+1197) of which we are informed through polemic references in the other canonists. Tancred and Bazianus were not the only ones who departed from the doctrine which considered the problem of the forced oath in the light of the matter comprised in the oath. Peter of Blois (+ after 1180) also rejected the distinction which was based on the elements of the *licitum* and the *illicitum,* giving as his reason the fact that the same decision would have been reached even if no *coactio* were involved. But he substituted the no less irrelevant distinction based on the *culpa praecedens.*[79]

Tancred and Bazianus, on the other hand, rejected the common theory along with its incidental deviations of doctrine and substituted a real consideration for the *coactio,* namely, the teaching of Roman Law about *metus.* Bazianus, who referred to the pretor as speaking *tanquam divina voce* when he gave the edict: "*Quod metus causa factum erit, ratum non habebo,*" held that the application of this principle should be invoked in order to as-

corporalem licet quod alias non liceret." This work is cited from Kuttner, *Schuldlehre,* pp. 299-333.

[78] Alanus, ad c. 4, *Comp.* I, *de iureiurando.* Damasus *(Quaestiones, de iureiurando):* "Item queritur de illa decretali 'Si vero aliquis', utrum sc. metu extortum sacramentum teneat, si aliquis per metum, qui posset cadere in constantem virum, renunciet iuri suo . . . Solutio: dicendum est, quod teneat, si habuerit animum faciendi hoc quod iurabat ille qui iuravit, licet quidam notaverint contra." Joannes Teutonicus, *Glossa ad Compilationem Tertiam, ad* c. 3, *de iureiurando.* These two last mentioned works are cited from Kuttner, *Schuldlehre,* pp. 299-333. Tancred, *Glossa Ordinaria ad Compilation Tertiam, ad* c. 3, *de iureiurando.*

[79] Petrus Blesensis, *Speculum Iuris Canonici* (Reimarus, Berlin, 1837) c. 42. This work is cited from Kuttner, *Schuldlehre,* pp. 299-333.

suage the harsher demand contained in the papal decretal.[80] Hence the *iuramentum metu extortum* was not to be considered binding, and its violation was consequently not imputable, provided that the fear was one *quod caderet in constantem virum.* Of course the fact of being forced offered no excuse for an assertory oath, for perjury had to be avoided in any circumstances.[81]

It is only in regard to the promissory oath that Bazianus and Tancred opposed the strictness of the common canonical teaching. And even in this respect Tancred, who in his *Glossa ad Compilationem Primam* and his *Glossa ad Compilationem Secundam* had followed Bazianus completely, later modified his stand in his *Glossa ad Compilationem Tertiam.* Here the *metus qui possit cadere in constantem virum* excused the victim only if he had no intention of fulfilling the oath inasmuch as he took the oath only to save himself.[82] This doctrine practically implied a return to the ideas of Alan († probably after 1238) and Damasus († after 1216) in spite of the difference of starting points.[83]

80 Tancredus *(Glossa Ordinaria ad Compilationem Primam, ad* c. 4, *de iureiurando.* [as also *Glossa Ordinaria ad Compilationem Secundam, ad* c. 6, h.t.]): "Baz. dixit,—cuius opinionem amplector—quod iuramentum metu seu vi extortum neminem obligat, (cum) tanquam divina voce pretor edixerit 'Quod metus causa factum erit, ratum non habebo' . . . A (lanus) et quidam alii notaverunt hic, quod si is qui metu iurat, habet animum adimplendi, obligatur, si non habet animum adimplendi, non obligatur . . . tertii (refers to Huguccio) dicunt, quod semper est obligatorium iuramentum metu extortum, quia est voluntarium licet metus precedat . . . set prius dictum magis michi placet . . . "

81 *Glossa Codicis G. (ad* c. 1, C. XV, q. 6): "Hinc oritur questio, si aliquis iuraverit coactus, quod res suas daret, an illud iuramentum sit obligatorium . . . B(azianus) non distinguit, dicens: si iuravit non tenetur, quia potest se tueri 'quod metus causa' . . . " This work is cited from Kuttner, *Schuldlehre,* pp. 299-333. Tancredus *(Glossa Ordinaria ad Compilationem Secundam, ad.* c. 6, *de iureiurando): "* . . . set prius dictum magis michi placet, quod iuramentum metu extortum non sit obligatorium, dummodo sit italis metus, qui cadit in constantem virum . . . quod locum habet in promissoriis iuramentis, secus in assertoriis, ad que falso facienda nulla condicione debet aliquis induci."

82 Tancredus, *Glossa Ordinaria ad Compilationem Tertiam, ad* c. 3, *de iureiurando.*

83 Cf. *supra,* pp. 20-22.

The problems of interpretation that resulted in the single actual cases given in the sources can only be indicated here. The majority of the decretals concerned with this question dealt with clerics who had been forced by threats to renounce under oath their benefices and other rights.[84] Some of the glossators, according to their fundamental idea on the licitness of such oaths, declared that the renunciation by oath was not allowed and hence was *ipso iure* ineffective, and that the papal absolution mentioned in the decretals was therefore only declaratory in character.[85] Others maintained that such a renunciation was allowed, and hence the absolution was necessary and effective *(constitutive),* and if it was not pronounced there remained a right to reclaim the benefice only by way of analogy with the pretorial restitution.[86] In like manner, if the act of resignation from the benefice was corroborated with an oath not to demand it back, such an oath could normally be regarded as not having any valid effect and hence the cleric could re-enter upon the possession of the benefice. But even if the oath was regarded as having a valid effect, then the cleric could obtain

[84] C. 2, C. XV, q. 6 (Nicholas II to the Bishops of Gaul, written between the years 1059-1061-JL, n. 4447; c. 2, *Comp.* I; c. 1, *Comp.* II; c. 1, *Comp.* III, *de his quae vi metusve causa fiunt* (cc. 2-4, X, *h.t.)* (Alexander III to the Bishop of Worcester, written between the years 1159-1181-JL, n. 14131; Clement III to the Bishop of Ely, England, written between the years 1187-1191-JL, n. 16572; Innocent III to the Bishop, Dean and Subdean of Lincoln, England, Feb. 5, 1200-Potthast, n. 946.); cc. 4, 9, *Comp. I;* c. 6, *Comp. II, de iureiurando* (cc. 8, 2, 15, X, *h.t.)* (Alexander III to the Bishop of Glasgow and the Canons of the same diocese, Feb. 21, 1173-JL, n. 12193; Gregory VII to the Bishop of Verdun and the Monastery of St. Salvator Septimiani, Jan. 10, 1078, also to Guilbert, Archbishop of Ravenna, Jan. 28, 1078-JK, nn. 3880, 3881; Celestine III to the Archbishop of Nidaros (Trondheim), Norway, written between the years 1191-1198-JL, n. 17639.

[85] *Summa Lipsiensis* (c. 1186) *(ad* c. 2, C. XV, q. 6): " . . . et dici potest, quod illicitum fuit iuramentum, . . . sic ergo litteram: 'absolvimus,' *i.e.,* absolutos ostendimus." Tancredus (+1235) *(Glossa Ordinaria ad Compilationem Secundam, ad* c. 6, *de iureiurando, v. absolverunt):* "i.e., absolutos ostenderunt, vel non ligatos . . . "

[86] Joannes Teutonicus (+1245) *(Glossa Ordinaria ad* c. 2, C. XV, q. 6): " . . . solvat et postea repetat."

from the Pope a relaxation of his oath and employ the papal grant to recover possession of the benefice.[87]

There was also another difficulty in regard to the "Hubaldus" case as decided by St. Augustine. St. Augustine had declared that the extorted promise of marriage was binding in this instance.[88] But this contradicted the canonical demands regarding the required freedom of the marital consent, which freedom excluded the recognition of any binding power as inherent in the sworn promise or the oath to contract marriage.[89] Here the decretists gave various answers. They said that there was question of an exceptional case, since the state of necessity for Hubaldus was occasioned by his own guilt. Or, perhaps Hubaldus declared a free-will consent later on. Again, if the oath was binding, its relaxation could have been requested. Finally, some interpreted the case to imply that St. Augustine may not have wanted to give a *preceptum* at all in consequence of which the marriage was to be regarded as valid for the clause *"matrimonium sit firmum et stabile"* could well be considered as only a counsel to contract a valid marriage in consideration of the oath.[90] It was only by means of such interpretations that a concordance of the canons in

[87] Tancredus *(Glossa Ordinaria ad Compilationem Secundam, ad* c. 1, *de his quae vi):* " . . . non obstante illa renuntiatione vel etiam iuramento illam repetere potest . . . " Joannes Teutonicus *(Glossa ad Compilationem Tertiam, ad* c. 1, *de his quae vi metusve causa fiunt):* "Set quid si iurasset non repetere? tunc non repeteret. . . . papa vero ex officio suo mandabit restitui. . . . impetrare etiam potest relaxationem iuramenti . . . et sic non obstante aliquo iuramento potest denunciare ecclesie factum . . . "

[88] Cf. *supra,* p. 15.

[89] Cf. c. 19, *Comp. I;* c. 2, *Comp. II, de sponsalibus, IV,* 1 (cc. 14-15, X, *h.t.).* Simon of Bisignano *(Glossa ad Decretum, ad* c. 22, C. XXII, q. 4): " . . . licet enim secundum leges coacta voluntas sit voluntas, non tamen voluntas talis est, que matrimonium faciat, cum enim matrimonium sine consensu non possit contrahi." According to Joannes Teutonicus, the four cases in which a forced oath did not bind were *votum, traditio rei ecclesiasticae, dos, matrimonium (Glossa Ordinaria ad Decretum, ad* c. 22, C. XXII, q. 4; *Glossa ad Compilationem Tertiam, ad* c. 3, *de iureiurando).*

[90] Rufinus (+1190) *(ad* c. 22, C. XXII, q. 4): " . . . (ut) tamen quia sua gravi culpa incidit in hanc necessitatem, merito teneatur eam accipere, quam prius coactus iuraverat . . . vel forte, quam prius compulsus iuraverat,

harmony with the scientific ideal of the time could be essayed.

This period which had seen the introduction of the clear Roman Law concepts of force and fear, and during which these terms had been discussed in relation to the validity and obligation of various legal actions, closed with the same disregard for a thorough consideration of the problem of fear as was noted in the preceding pages. As noted, there were a few individual authors who were exceptions to this rule. The following article will trace the development of the doctrine of the canonists on this subject through the next period, which starts with the decretals of Gregory IX (1234).

Article II. Gregory IX to the Council of Trent

In the preceding period the categories of *vis* and *metus, coactio absoluta* and *coactio conditionalis* were definitely and clearly established in the doctrine of the canonists. The present period which extends for some three hundred years, from about the middle of the 13th century until the middle of the 16th century, did not bring many important changes in the canonical doctrine on the excusing effect of force and fear. There was hardly any new positive legislation on this subject and so the discussion among the canonists continued along the same lines as in the period following the *Decretum Gratiani.*

The decretals of Gregory IX contain only one new canon under the title *De his quae vi metusve causa fiunt.*[91] The other six canons are already found in one or the other of the previous compilations and have been commented upon in the foregoing section. Moreover, since this canon of Gregory treats merely a case of procedural law, it is not of importance in the question of imputability. In the *Liber Sextus* of Boniface VIII (1298), the title *De his quae vi*

postea volens acceperat . . . ". Huguccio (+1210) *(ad* c. 22, C. XXII, q. 4): " . . . cum ergo iste, licet coactus, iuraverit eam accipere in uxorem, et hoc potest facere sine peccato, debet ad hoc cogi ab ecclesia . . . set quia coactus iuravit hoc, et quia consensus maritalis voluntarius et spontaneus debet esse, si de nolente non efficitur volens, set semper denegat, absolvendus est . . . "

[91] C. 7, X, *de his quae vi metusve causa fiunt,* I, 40,—Gregory IX, written between the years 1227-1234—Potthast, n. 9576.

metusve causa fiunt contains only one decretal, and it adds nothing that is essentially new to the doctrine on imputability.[92]

I. THE GENERAL TEACHING, TERMINOLOGY

The Roman Law terms were now used generally. Nevertheless the glossators at times interchanged the terms "*coactio absoluta*" and "*vis*", "*coactio conditionalis*" and "*metus*".[93] They adhered quite strictly to the Roman Law definitions.[94] The terms "*probabilis*" *and* "*non-probabilis*" are now used as synonymous with "*iustus*" and "*iniustus*" or "*vanus.*"[95] St. Raymond of Penyafort (+ 1275) divided *coactio* or *vis* into a *levis* and a *violenta coactio.* Similarly he divided *metus* into *metus qui cadit in constantem virum* and *qui non cadit.*[96]

Coactio Conditionalis

St. Raymond, like Bernard of Pavia,[97] explained the objective norm of the *vir constans* by a subjective norm, namely, the par-

[92] C. un., *de his quae vi metusve causa fiunt,* I, 20, in VI° (Gregory X to the Council of Lyons): "Absolutionis beneficium, ab excommunicationis sententia vel quamcumque revocationem ipsius, aut suspensionis, seu etiam interdicti per vim vel metum extorta: praesentis constitutionis auctoritate omnino viribus vacuamus. Ne autem sine vindicta violentiae crescat audacia: eos, qui absolutionem seu revocationem huiusmodi vi vel metu extorserint, excommunicationis sententiae decernimus subiacere."

[93] Cf., e.g., Bernardus Parmensis (+1266), *Glossa Ordinaria* ad c. 5, X, *de his quae vi metusve causa fiunt,* I, 40.

[94] Cf., e.g., Bernardus Parmensis, *Glossa Ordinaria ad* c. 4, X, *de his quae vi metusve causa fiunt,* I, 40; Cardinalis Hostiensis (Henricus de Segusio) (+1271), *Commentaria in Quinque Decretalium Libros* (5 vols. in 3, Venetiis, 1581), ad c. 2, X, *de his quae vi metusve causa fiunt,* I, 40 (hereafter referred to as Hostiensis-*Lectura);* Hostiensis, *Summa Aurea* (Lugduni, 1568), Tit. I, *De his quae vi metusve causa fiunt,* (I, 40) #1, f. 93 v; Ioannes Andreae (+1348), *Glossa Ordinaria ad* c. 1, *de his quae vi metusve causa fiunt, I,* 20, in VI°. Hostiensis, *Summa Aurea (loc. cit.):* "Dicitur metus, quasi mentem scil. liberam tenens, id est retinens, seu impediens: nam qui timorem habet non quod ore semper exprimit mente gerit."

[95] E.g., Hostiensis, *(Summa Aurea,* Tit. *De his quae vi metusve causa fiunt,* [I, 40] #2, f. 93 v.): "... non probabilis est, quando cadit in miserum hominem securum."

[96] *Summa* Tit. *De impedimento violentiae sive metus* (Lib. IV, Tit. IV), p. 505.

[97] Cf. *supra,* p. 13.

ticular circumstances attending an individual person.[98] But once again the other canonists concentrated on the abstract standard of the *vir constans* and studied to gauge the amount of fear which he must be expected to resist and which he cannot be expected to resist. Thus Bernard of Parma in the *Glossa Ordinaria* to the decretals of Gregory listed fear of death, of rape, of enslavement, or of blows as nullifying the canonical effects of a vow.[99] But they also admitted a subjective norm to some extent. Thus Bernard of Parma in his *Glossa Ordinaria* to c. 14, X, *De sponsalibus et matrimoniis*, IV, I stated: "A lesser fear excuses a woman more than it excuses a man." [100]

Here again one notes the question of the *culpa praecedens* coming to the fore. Bernard of Parma insisted that if on the side of the victim a *culpa praecedens* was involved, then the victim was not to be given any legal protection or aid, except in the cases of matrimony, of a dowry promised through fear or already bestowed, of church property given or promised by oath through fear, of a vow, of jurisdiction extorted through fear, and of the authority of a tutor similarly extorted.[101] Hostiensis added a few more cases

[98] *Summa* (Tit. *De impedimento violentiae sive metus* [Lib. IV, Tit. IV], p. 506: "Item nota quod talis caderet in unum, qui non diceretur cadere in alium; quia non est verisimile hominem clarae dignitatis in urbe timuisse, vel quod Rex parvi militis metu timeat."

[99] *Ad* c. 1, X, *de his quae vi metusve causa fiunt,* I, 40. Similarly Hostiensis *(Lectura, ad.* c. 6, X, *de his quae vi metusve causa fiunt,* I, 40 *ad v. nec metu mortis)*: " . . . invenio quod excusat metus amissionis rerum. item metus impediendae promotionis. item onerandae libertatis. item iudicis. item verberum. item suspicio metus. item excommunicationis. Cf. Ioannes Andreae Bononiensis, *In Primum Decretalium Librum Commentaria* (Venetiis, apud Franciscum Franciscium Senensem, 1581) (hereafter referred to as *'Novellae')*, *ad* c. 6, X, *de his quae vi metusve causa fiunt,* I, 40.

[100] "Minor tamen metus magis excusat feminam, quam virum. Cf. also Ioannes Andreae, *Novellae ad* c. 6, X, *de his quae vi metusve causa fiunt,* I, 40, *ad v. et ibi arbitrio.*

[101] *Glossa Ordinaria (ad* c. 2, X, *de his quae vi metusve causa fiunt,* I, 40): " . . . Tenent ergo quae per metum fiunt et subvenitur passus, nisi culpa sua incidit in metum. Ab ista doctrina sive generalitate, excipitur casus in quibus fallit etiam si culpa incidisset in metum. Et primo in causa matrimonii qualiscumque metus interveniat culpa sua vel sine culpa, matri-

in which the effects of a fear-inspired act were invalid even though a *culpa praecedens* was involved on the side of the victim. He also considered the case whether a threat of excommunication gave rise to a *metus probabilis*. He concluded that in consequence of the temporal as well as the spiritual harm involved such an occasioned fear was to be regarded *probabilis*.[102]

Towards the end of the previous period there was an emergence of more lenient opinions regarding the effects of actions performed under fear.[103] For the present period there is noticeable a recurrence of the strict theory of the imputability of actions committed under fear, founded on the phase *"Coacta voluntas est voluntas"*, which theory allowed no excuse for a crime committed under fear as long as a mortal sin was involved.[104] But Hostiensis in his *Lectura* followed the distinction which Alan had formulated in regard to oaths, applying this to the general teaching on the imputability of actions. He distinguished the *forum Dei* and the

monium contractum per metum non tenet . . . Item et dos promissa per metum vel soluta non tenet; . . . Item in rebus ecclesiae . . . Item et in voto . . . Item non tenet jurisdictio per metum extorta . . . Item auctoritas tutoris . . . In omnibus aliis tenet: dum tamen talia sunt, quae sine interitu salutis aeternae servari possint . . .

> Tutor, iudicium, dos, sacrum, copula, votum
> Haec sex in vi facta de iure scias fore nulla
> Cetera ius patitur, sed postea restituitur.

102 *Lectura (ad* c. 2, X, *de his quae vi metusve causa fiunt,* I, 40): "Nisi qui in metum incidat culpa sua, tunc enim non subvenitur . . . Excipiuntur tamen casus in quibus etsi qui in metum culpa sua incideret, subvenitur . . . in testamenti factione . . . in sententiae pronunciatione . . . in procuratoris constitutione . . . in aliis autem tenet mero iure, quod agitur, sed metum passus subvenitur. *Idem (op. cit. ad* c. 6, X, *de his quae vi metusve causa fiunt,* 1, 40; *ad v. Nec metum mortis):* " . . .Item excommunicationis. nec mirum quia continet nedum corporis sed et animae detrimentum. Nec obest si dicas medicinalis est: quia hoc verum est, quando causa subest et quando etiam non subest propter bonum obedientiae. Verumtamen nollet hanc recipere medicinam; quia haec medicina multoties plus aufert, quam afferat."

103 Cf. *supra*, pp. 13, 14, Alan and Tancred.

104 E.g., Bernardus Parmensis, *Glossa Ordinaria, ad* c. 2, X, *de his quae vi metusve causa fiunt,* I, 40.

forum ecclesiae, and held that a grave fear excused its victim from judicial sentence and punishment, but not from interior guilt.[105]

Ioannes Andreae (+ 1348), on the other hand, argued against Hostiensis that, while a *coactio absoluta (vis)* excused its victim from fault and punishment, a *coactio conditionalis (metus)* indeed lessened the gravity of the fault but did not free the victim from punishment.[106] In discussing the types of *metus* in question in the decretal of Innocent III (1198-1216),[107] Ioannes Andreae quoted Innocent IV (1243-1254) as saying that some claimed that the *coactio conditionalis* or *metus* there mentioned was a *metus vanus.* Ioannes Andreae agreed with Innocent IV and Hostiensis that the *metus* in question was a *metus iustus,* but he then also considered the influence of the *metus vanus.* He concluded that such a *metus* when seizing upon a timid soul *(meticulosus)* lessened the culpability of the act, for the victim of such a fear harbored less contempt for the law which he violated than the one who acted freely, and therefore he also sinned less grievously.[108] This was the first time that a major commentator admitted explicitly that a *metus vanus* lessened culpability. But it must be noted that a *metus vanus* of this early period was the equivalent of the present-day *metus relative gravis,* for the canonists of this period did not even consider the *metus levis* in its modern acceptation. However, the argument used by Ioannes Andreae regarding *metus vanus* could in a measure be applied likewise to *metus levis* as this latter term is used today.

II. RESULTS OF A FORCED OATH

In the later decretals themselves there is nothing to change the doctrine of Canon Law with regard to forced oaths, their binding

[105] *Lectura (ad* c. 5, X, *de his quae vi metusve causa fiunt,* I, 40, *ad v. cum pro nullo metu):* " . . . licet excusat a sententia et poena, ut ibi, non tamen a culpa ut hic."

[106] *Novella (ad* c. 5, X, *de his quae vi metusve causa fiunt,* I, 40): "Metus conditionalis non excusat ab excommunicatione communionis, ut hic, nec ab irregularitate rebaptizationis . . . nec a periurio, . . . sed omni casu, quod si iustus est, i.e. qui potuit cadere in constantem, culpa attenuat, ut hic."

[107] C. 5, X, *de his quae vi metusve causa fiunt,* I, 40.

[108] *Novella ad* c. 5, X, *de his quae vi metusve causa fiunt,* I, 40.

force or the imputability attaching to the neglect of their fulfillment. However, these questions were discussed at some length by the canonists of this period, but without their coming to any entirely new conclusions.

Bernard of Parma (+ 1266) in his *Glossa Ordinaria* to the decretals of Gregory IX disregarded the teaching of canonists like Bazianus (+1197), Alan (+ probably after 1238) and Tancred (+1235).[109] He insisted on the imputability of the breaking of any oath whose content was licit and qualified this opinion only with *"non punitur pro mortali"*.[110] Hostiensis (+1271) likewise followed this strict opinion.[111] However, he indicated a way in which one who renounced, for example, a benefice under fear, could recover its possession no matter what type of oath he had taken when he resigned it under the duress of fear. In this Hostiensis developed a solution proposed by the earlier authors, as was seen above.[112] Hostiensis pointed out that a cleric could obtain a relaxation of his oath or, if he had sworn not to petition for this, he could at least denounce the act of violence to the church authorities. He would then be absolved from the obligation of the oath *motu proprio.*[113] Finally Ioannes Andreae followed the same

[109] Cf. *supra*, pp. 20-23.

[110] *Glossa Ordinaria ad* cc. 2, 3, 6, X, *de his quae vi metusve causa fiunt,* I, 40; cc. 8, 15, X, *de iureiurando,* II. 24.

[111] *Lectura (ad* c. 3, X, *de his quae vi metusve causa fiunt,* I, 40 *ad v. confirmata):* " . . . sed turpiter tantum praestitum, i.e. dolo vel metu extortum, et tale obligat." Cf. *Summa Aurea,* Tit. *De his quae vi metusve causa fiunt,* #5 *(additio)* (I, 40) f. 94 v.

[112] Cf. *supra*, p. 24.

[113] *Summa Aurea (loc. cit.):* " . . . Sed refert utrum iuraverit quis resignare tantum, vel etiam non repetere; si iuraverit tantum resignare illud servandum est, sed tamen directe ipso beneficio resignato potest rescriptum impetrare et ipsum repetere per actionem quod met. causa. quae in rem datur licet personalis sit, . . . Si vero iuraverit non repetere. et iterum sibi conferatur recipere potest, et ex secunda receptione agere . . . Item absolutus per Papam poterit petere ex prima institutione, sic potest intelligi dictum capit. cum inter [c. 2, X, *de renunciatione,* I, 9] . . . Quid si iuraverit non venire contra iuramentum id est non petere absolutionem, adhuc potest ecclesiae nuntiare, et ecclesia ad nunciationem ipsius ipsum absolvere motu proprio . . . Si vero iuravit [non] denuntiare non valet . . . Sed verum est quo ad

strict opinion which derived its conclusions in view of the elements of licitness and illicitness in the content of the forced oath. He based his opinion on the teaching of Innocent IV in this regard.[114]

The teaching of Ioannes Andreae furnishes a fundamentally complete idea of the canonical doctrine on force and fear as it was current at the end of this period. The final conclusions of the decretists and the decretalists were in a certain sense crystallized in his writings. He insisted on the strict opinion according to which only a *coactio absoluta* excused its victim from fault, while the *coactio conditionalis,* though it mitigated the fault to some extent, did not free its victim from punishment. His consideration of the rôle of *metus vanus* (i.e. relatively grave fear) as also lessening the fault may well be the foundation for its consideration along similar lines by the later canonists. He thus also indirectly introduced the question of *metus levis,* as this term is understood today. Finally, his strict opinion regarding the forced oath revealed little if any departure from the teaching of the earlier canonists like Huguccio.

The conclusion which Kuttner draws regarding the stabilized canonical doctrine as it existed at the end of the period between Gratian and Gregory IX may well be accepted in regard also to the entire period of the *Corpus Iuris Canonici.* He notes that there was a common disregard for any thoroughgoing consideration of the *coactio conditionalis,* except in the case of a few individual authors. Most of the canonists of that period repeatedly applied the phrase *"Coacta voluntas est voluntas",* and were unrelenting in their assertion of guilt in forced actions of the will, even though the threat of death was employed. It was only in practice that this concept was mitigated, as was evidenced in the

paenitentiam peragendam. Sed si qui iuravit zelo rei recuperandae ad denunciationem faciendam, quam zelo animae proximi videtur sanum esse consilium quod non denuntiet, quia iam deieraret, ergo in hoc casu amico eget, secundum hos intellige infra de iurejur. cap. primo [c. 1, X; *de iureiurando,* II, 24] et cap. debitores [c. 6, X, *de iureiurando,* II, 24]. Sic ergo omne sacramentum tenendum nisi vergat in dispendium salutis aeternae, nam tunc tenendum non est."

[114] *Novella ad* c. 3, X, *de his quae vi metusve causa fiunt,* I, 40, *v. spoliatus.*

granting of absolutions, mitigations of punishment, and forensic helps.[115] Just as there was a reaction against the more lenient doctrines of Tancred (+1235) and Bazianus (+1197) as evidenced in the *Glossa Ordinaria* of Bernard of Parma (+1266) at the close of the preceding period, so also in the *Novellae* of Ioannes Andreae (+1348), whose opinions reflect the canonical teaching at the end of this period, there was a certain reaction against the moderately liberal opinions of Hostiensis (+1271).

[115] *Schuldlehre*, p. 333.

CHAPTER II

FROM THE COUNCIL OF TRENT TO THE CODE OF CANON LAW

ARTICLE I. THE INFLUENCE OF MORAL THEOLOGY

The development of the doctrine on force and fear during this period is almost entirely independent of any new positive legislation on the part of the Church. The last piece of legislation on this point is contained in the decretal of Gregory X (1271-1276) issued at the II General Council of Lyons (1274),[1] which has been referred to above.[2] And it is not until the Constitution *Apostolicae Sedis* of Pius IX (Oct. 12, 1869) [3] that any legislation directly affected the rôle of force and fear as excusing factors in penal law. Moreover, court proceedings were limited almost exclusively to clerical cases. But many, if not most of the clerical cases were handled in an administrative way, with the result that there was practically no important court jurisprudence respecting force and fear in relation to the imputability attaching to delictual acts.

The moralists who draw upon the doctrine of such Scholastics of the 13th century as Alexander of Hales (+1245), St. Thomas (+1274) St. Bonaventure (+1274) and John Duns Scotus (+1308) were responsible for almost all the development in the post Tridentine period. Through these same Scholastics the distinctions of Aristotle regarding the degree of willfulness in an act done from fear found their way into moral treaties. Although the canonists contemporaneous with St. Thomas and St. Bonaventure did not incorporate the findings of these Scholastics in their own canonical commentaries, later canonists, especially those of the 16th and 17th centuries, availed themselves of the developments that had taken

[1] C. un., *de his quae vi metusve causa fiunt,* I, 20, in VI°.

[2] Cf. pp. 26-27.

[3] *Codicis Iuris Canonici Fontes cura Emi. Petri Card. Gasparri Editi* (9 vols., Romae [postea Civitate Vaticana]: Typis Polyglottis Vaticanis, 1923-1939, [Vols. VII, VIII, *et* IX ed. *cura et studio Emi. Iustiniani Card. Serédi*]). n. 552. This work will be cited as *Fontes.*

place in moral theology due to the influence of these Scholastics. The binding force of the juridical norms thus developed depended on the general acceptance of the Church through custom.[4] The title *"De his quae vi metusve causa fiunt"* under which Bernard of Pavia and the later compilers grouped the decretals concerning the matter of compulsion was still retained by many of the canonists of this period. However, following the lead of the moralists, they treated the doctrine according to the scholastic method of definition, division and statement of principles.[5]

The definitions and divisions of *vis* and *metus* which had been clearly set forth by the canonists after Alexander III (1159-1181)[6] remained almost unchanged throughout this period. However, certain new concepts gradually worked their way into these distinctions due to the influence of the Scholastics of the 13th century. Alexander of Hales, whose *Summa* was the first to appear after the complete introduction of Aristotle's works to scholastic thought, added the notion of discretion to that of the *vir constans*. Thus he defined *metus probabilis* as that which results from a cause which can affect a "resolute and discreet man."[7]

St. Thomas Aquinas likewise stressed the need of considering the quality of discretion in a *vir constans*. He classified a resolute man as reflecting the golden mean between the two extremes of irresolution and stubbornness in man. A resolute man thus was defined as one who first follows right reason in choosing whether or not to submit to the demands of a threat, and thus always

[4] Cf. Hinschius, *Das Kirchenrecht der Katholiken und Protestanten in Deutschland* (6 vols., Berlin, 1869-1879), V, 923-924.

[5] V. gr., Barbosa, *Collectanea Doctorum tam Veterum quam Recentorum in Jus Pontificium Universum* (5 vols., Lugduni 1637) lib. I, tit. XL (hereafter cited as Barbosa); Pirhing, *Jus Canonicum in Libros Decretalium* (5 vols., Dilingae, 1722), lib. I. tit. XL (hereafter cited as Pirhing); Reiffenstuel, *Jus Canonicum Universum* (4 vols., Venetiis, 1735), lib. I, tit. XL (hereafter cited as Reiffenstuel); Schmalzgrueber, *Jus Ecclesiasticum Universum* (5 vols. in 12, Romae, 1843-1845), lib. I, tit. XL (hereafter cited as Schmalzgrueber).

[6] Cf. *supra*, p. 10.

[7] *Summa Theologiae* (ed. PP. Collegii S. Bonaventurae, 3 vols.., Ad Claras Aquas: Typographia Collegii S. Bonaventurae. 1924-1930), lib. III, inq. III, tract VI, qu. II, tit. I, cap. 6.

chooses to undergo the lesser evil in order to escape the greater.[8] St. Thomas borrowed this concept from Aristotle's description of the intrepid man,[9] and thereby helped to perfect the old Roman Law concept which had been adopted by the earlier writers.

St. Bonaventure, on the other hand, simply taught that a just fear was present in the fear of death, of mutilation, of servitude or of assault, which must be recognized as affecting even a resolute man when he assumes that the one who perpetrates the threat can and will in all probability also execute it.[10]

Scotus maintained much the same notion of the *vir constans* as St. Bonaventure. Thus, for grave fear he required two conditions; first, the evil must be grave in itself, and secondly, it must really threaten one, the threat being at least morally certain. If either of these conditions was lacking, Scotus term the fear *levis*.[11]

These distinctions and concepts of the Scholastics were not all accepted by the canonists in exactly the same form, but the reasoning of the Scholastics did bring about a new approach to the problem of imputability, and of the validity of acts performed under stress of force or fear. Sporer (+1683), one of the great moralists

[8] *Scriptum in Quartum Sententiarum Magistri Petri Lombardi—Opera Omnia,* (Venetiis, 1595), Vol. VII, dist. XXIX, q. 1, art. I.

[9] *Nichomachean Ethics—The Basic Works of Aristotle,* (edited by R. McKeon, New York: Random House, 1941), Book III, c. I (n. 1110a).

[10] *Commentaria in Quatuor Libros Sententiarum Magistri Petri Lombardi —Opera Omnia,* (ed. PP. Collegii S. Bonaventurae, 8 vols., Ad Claras Aquas: Typographia Collegii S. Bonaventurae, 1892-1898), lib. IV *in Quartum Librum Magistri, dist. XXIX, art I, q. 1.*

[11] *Quaestiones in Quartum Librum Sententiarum—Opera Omnia,* (26 vols., Parisiis, 1891-1895) Vol. XIX, dist. XXIX, q. un.

A similar division of fear is found in the writings of the Oriental canonists at this time. Chomatianus (Demetrius, + ca. 1234) stated: "Dicendum vero hic legem illum agnoscere metum, qui non quidem apparens, sed realis est: etenim metum apparentem etiam Divina Scriptura tamquam non existentem existimat, asserit enim: 'Quoniam trepidaverunt timore ubi non erat timor'. Metum vero realem iurisprudentia dividit in illum qui poenam affert sive mortiferum, et in levem sive sine periculo."—*Analecta,* ed. Pitra, Tomus VII, coll. 459 (as quoted by Isidorus Croce, *Textus Selecti ex operibus Commentatorum Byzantinorum Iuris Ecclesiastici,* Fonti, Serie II, Fascicolo V, Civitate Vaticana: Typis Polyglottis Vaticanis, 1939.)

of the 17th century, stressed the further distinction of *metus ab intrinseco* and *metus ab extrinseco* to aid in the clarification of the problem of fear. He was also one of the first moralists to use the term "*metus reverentialis,*" which he described as being *levis* if considered abstractly, but often *gravis* in a concrete instance.[12]

The canonists were not long in following the lead of the moralists regarding these distinctions. Pirhing (1606-1679) also discussed the importance of *metus reverentialis,* and clearly set forth the distinction between absolutely and relatively grave fear, using these precise terms.[13] Reiffenstuel (1641-1703), who followed Scotus (1266-1308) in his definition of *metus gravis,* requiring objective gravity in the thing threatened as well as moral certitude that it will happen, demanded also in regard to contracts that the fear be inflicted in order to compel consent, and that otherwise the contract is not valid or rescissible.[14]

Finally, Schmalzgrueber (1663-1735) gave the most complete division of any of the canonists, logically distinguishing the various notions of fear contributed by the earlier moralists and canonists. He has a threefold division of fear: (1) by reason of its cause, that which is inflicted by either an intrinsic or an extrinsic necessary cause, such as sickness or shipwreck and that which is inflicted by a free created cause, such as the threats of a man; (2) by reason of the manner in which it is inflicted, that which is either justly or unjustly inflicted. The latter in turn is unjustly inflicted either to exact a promise, a contract or the like, or it is inflicted for some other purpose; (3) by reason of its quality, that which is grave or slight. Grave fear is either absolutely grave or relatively grave.[15]

In determining the requirements for grave fear, this author was perhaps the most detailed of all canonists. He demanded five requisites, namely, that it be fear of a certain grave evil and not of an

[12] *Theologia Moralis Decalogalis et Sacramentalis* (ed. I Bierbaum, 3 vols., Paderbornae, 1897-1901), I, nn. 155, 157 (hereafter cited as *Theologia Moralis*).

[13] Lib. I. tit. XL, n. VI, assertio VI.

[14] Lib. I, tit. XL, nn. 19, 28.

[15] Lib. I, tit. XL, n. 2.

indefinite evil; that the one threatening the fear can easily execute his threat or be believed capable of doing so; that such a one is wont to execute his threats or is reasonably feared to execute them; that the one threatened cannot easily escape the evil; and finally that the victim really believes the evil to be grave. Schmalzgrueber claimed that any fear which did not have these five requisites was not a grave fear with respect to the one threatened.[16]

The glossator Laurentius (+after 1212) had introduced the Aristotelian distinction of *voluntarium simpliciter* and *voluntarium secundum quid* into canonistic thought.[17] But the more general discussion, among the Scholastics, of the degree of imputability according to the terms "*voluntarium simpliciter*" and "*voluntarium secundum quid*" on the one hand, and "*involuntarium simpliciter*" and "*involuntarium secundum quid*" on the other, evidently stemmed from the writings of St. Thomas Aquinas. Thus St. Thomas dealt with the problem involved in the earlier axiom: "*Coacta voluntas est voluntas*" by means of this distinction drawn from Aristotle. Even the classic example of the storm-tossed voyager throwing his goods into the sea, which has found its way into practically all manuals of Moral Theology, was taken by St. Thomas from Aristotle's *Nicomachean Ethics*.[18] An act forced by violence is absolutely in-

[16] Lib. I, tit. XL, n. 3.

[17] Cf. Kuttner, *Schuldlehre*, p. 49.

[18] *Scriptum in Quartum Sententiarum*, dist. XXIX, q. 1, art. I; Aristotle, *Nicomachean Ethics* (Book III, c. I [n. 1110a]): "But with regard to the things that are done (e.g. if a tyrant were to order one to do something base, having one's parents and children in his power, and if one did the action they were to be saved, but otherwise would be put to death), it may be debated whether such actions are involuntary or voluntary. Something of the sort happens also with regard to the throwing of goods overboard in a storm, for in the abstract no one throws goods away voluntarily, but on condition of its securing the safety of himself and his crew any sensible man does so. Such actions, then, are mixed, but are more like voluntary actions; for they are worthy of choice at the time when they are done, and the end of an action is relative to the occasion. Both the terms, then, 'voluntary' and 'involuntary' must be used with reference to the moment of action. Now the man acts voluntarily; for the principle that moves the instrumental parts of the body in such actions is in him, and the things of which the moving

voluntary, while one induced through fear is *simpliciter voluntarium* and *involuntarium secundum quid.*[19]

Although this distinction added nothing essential to the axiom "*Coacta voluntas est voluntas,*" it did help in clarifying the teaching on imputability by stressing the involuntary content of such an act, showing it to be, as it were, a mixed act composed of a voluntary and an involuntary element. This later bore fruit in the clear teaching of such writers as Sporer, Reiffenstuel and Schmalzgrueber regarding the moral guilt of such actions.[20]

Article II. Influence of Force and Fear on Validity of Promises, Vows and Contracts

As pointed out above, the rôle of force and fear in penal law is in its historical development dependent to a great extent upon the canonical doctrine on force and fear in the field of contracts, promises and oaths. The Code itself still shows definite traces of this development in treating only of *metus ab extrinseco* under the term "*metus gravis*" in regard to imputability and responsibility. Consequently it was thought better to continue to follow the canonical doctrine on contracts, etc., through the entire pre-Code period.

At the close of the preceding period it had generally been held that grave fear ordinarily did not render the promise or contract void, but only voidable, and that only if there was no *culpa praecedens* involved.[21] Not long after the beginning of the post-Triden-

principle is in a man himself are in his power to do or not to do. Such actions, therefore, are voluntary, but in the abstract perhaps involuntary; for no one would choose any such act in itself."

[19] Cf. St. Thomas, *Scriptum in Quartum Sententiarum,* dist. XXIV, q. I, art. I.

[20] For the use of these terms cf. Sporer, *Theologia Moralis,* I, nn. 158, 160, 167; Pirhing, lib. I, tit. XL, nn. 2, 3; Laymann (1575-1635), *Theologia Moralis* (Venetiis, 1719), lib. I, tract II, cap. VI, n. 7; lib. III, tract. IV, cap. VI, n. 4; Schmalzgrueber, lib. I, tit. XL, nn. 1, 8, 11, 17, 23; St. Alphonsus Liguori (1696-1787), *Theologia Moralis* (ed. L. Gaudé, 4 vols., Romae: Typis Polyglottis Vaticanis, 1905-1912), lib. III, n. 197; Wernz (1842-1914), *Ius Decretalium* (6 vols., Romae et Prati, 1906 1913), VI, n. 526.

[21] Cf. *supra,* pp. 28-29.

tine period Laymann (1575-1635) reaffirmed this same teaching, but drew attention to the fact that fear *ab intrinseco* never rendered a contract either void or voidable. He also held that contracts extorted by a *metus levis* directly and unjustly inflicted were voidable. He called this the common teaching of his time. He argued that the reason for which grave fear renders a contract voidable is that it contains an injury in itself and a force directly aimed at extorting the consent of the other party, which consent is *secundum quid involuntarium*. Therefore, if the same conditions obtained regarding *metus levis,* it too offered a sufficient reason for the rescinding of a contract. However, Laymann explicitly excepted marriage and religious profession from these contracts, since he maintained that by positive church law marriage and religious profession were void when contracted with grave fear, precisely for the reason that once validly contracted they could not be dissolved. Since he did not clearly distinguish *metus absolute gravis* and *metus relative gravis,* he most probably included the latter under *metus levis,* as earlier canonists had done.[22] But his reasoning applied equally well to *metus levis* as accepted by later canonists, and applied also to slight fear in relation to delicts, for a delict committed *ex metu levi* was really *secundum quid involuntarium.*[23]

Pirhing (1606-1679), one of the first great canonists of this period, followed Laymann in this opinion on the validity of contracts.[24] Reiffenstuel (1641-1703) maintained that *metus levis* never rendered a contract voidable, giving as his reason the fact that it does not affect a resolute man.[25] Sporer (+1683) is one of the few who maintained against Laymann that contracts containing an obligation, promises and vows are void by the natural law when they are entered through grave, unjust fear.[26]

St. Alphonsus (1696-1787), though following Laymann regarding the voidability of contracts entered through grave fear, denied

[22] Cf. *supra,* p. 30; Ioannes Andreae, *Novella* ad. c. 5, X, *de his quae vi metusve causa fiunt,* I, 40.

[23] *Theologia Moralis,* lib. I, tract. II, cap. VI, nn. 5, 7, 8; lib. III, tract. IV, cap. VI, nn.1-5.

[24] Lib. I, tit. XL, nn. 5, 6, 7, 11, 13.

[25] Lib. I, tit. XL, n. 25.

[26] *Theologia Moralis,* I, n. 165, 166.

that *metus levis* was ever sufficient to render a contract rescissible. By this time a clear distinction had already been drawn between *metus absolute gravis, relative gravis,* and *levis.* Evidently, St. Alphonsus was referring only to *metus levis* in the modern acceptation, for he gave as his reason the fact that one was not presumed to have consented from fear, but rather freely, if he knew it was a a slight fear and could have rejected it, but did not do so. He also held that a vow taken out of grave fear unjustly inflicted was invalid by reason at least of ecclesiastical law.[27] Wernz maintained the voidability of a contract entered through grave fear, but denied it in the case of *metus levis,* although he explicitly conceded it in the case of *metus relative gravis.*[28]

Finally, all the canonists agreed that this excusing fear had to be unjustly inflicted by a free external agent. None admitted *metus ab intrinseco* as rendering any contract void or voidable as long as it does not deprive the agent of the use of his reason.[29]

Article III. Forced Oaths

At the end of the preceding period the strict opinion regarding the binding force and imputability of forced oaths as advanced by Hostiensis and Ioannes Andreae was common among the canonists. This teaching which had been taken from the early decretists was based on a differentiation between the licitness and illicitness of the forced oath, and held that the oath was binding as long as the subject matter was licit.[30] In the present period this same strict

[27] *Theologia Moralis,* lib. III, n. 718; lib. III, n. 197.

[28] *Ius Decretalium,* VI, nn. 528, 530.

[29] "Certum est . . . esse validos, nec rescissioni obnoxios actus, qui metu etiam gravi gesti sunt, si iste proveniat a principio intrinseco, vel extrinseco naturali non libero. Patet in votis, et juramentis, quae ab omnibus pro validis habentur, etsi facta sint timore mortis in gravi infirmitate, vel naufragio. Ratio est, quia causa unica, ob quam actus metu gesti irriti sunt, aut rescinduntur, est injuria, quae metum passo illatum est; hanc autem non patitur ille, qui patitur metum sibi illatum a causa non libera."—Schmalzgrueber, lib. I, tit. XL, n. 8; Cf. also Wernz, *Ius Decretalium,* VI, n. 530; Ferraris, *Bibliotheca, Canonica Iuridica Moralis Theologica necnon Ascetica Polemica Rubricistica Historica* (9 vols., Romae, 1885-1889) s. v. *metus,* n. 15 (hereafter cited *Bibliotheca); Pirhing, lib. I, tit. XL, n. 10.

[30] Cf. *supra,* pp. 31-32.

opinion was the dominant one,[31] but much of the reasoning on this subject was taken by the canonists from the moralists of this and the preceding period.

St. Bonaventure in his Commentary on the Book of Sentences had distinguished the obligation in the *forum ecclesiae* and in the *forum conscientiae.* He maintained that the forced promissory oath was not binding in the ecclesiastical forum, since the Church presumes that one who is forced to swear does not swear with the intention of fulfilling the oath, but rather of avoiding the danger, and also since the one who forces another to swear has acquired no right thereby and should not receive any benefit from his misdeed. However, in the forum of conscience it did bind.[32]

St. Thomas differentiated the obligation towards the one who forced the oath from the obligation towards God, in whose name something was thus promised. The one swearing under compulsion was in no way obliged to the one who was the author of this compulsion, but he was obliged to God and had to seek from competent authority a relaxing of this latter obligation.[33] Sporer explained this distinction of St. Thomas by stating that a forced oath obliged from the virtue of religion because of the reverence due the divine Name. And thus such an oath which was *simpliciter voluntarium,* although not sufficiently voluntary to bind out of justice, was nevertheless supposed to be sufficiently voluntary to bind by reason of the virtue of religion.[34]

[31] Cf., e.g., Barbosa, lib. I, tit. XL, ad c. 4; Pirhing, lib. I, tit. XL, n. 17.

[32] Tomus,III, dist. XXXIX, art. III, q. II: St. Bonaventure was here following the earlier canonists referred to above, pages 26-30. Cf. also Kuttner, Schuldlehre, pp. 323-325. St. Alphonsus follows this same line of reasoning in his *Theologia Moralis,* lib. III, n. 174.

[33] *Summa Theologica* (ed. Studii Generalis O. Pr., Ottawa, Canada, 1942) IIa-IIae, q. 89, art. 7 ad 3. Cajetan (1469-1534) in commenting on this teaching of St. Thomas mentioned but rejected the opinion of some who held that such an oath bound only under venial sin if it was taken in consequence of really grave fear.—*Commentaria ad Doctoris Angelici Opera Omnia iussu impensaque Leonis XIII, P. M. edita* (Romae, 1882—; IIa IIae, (Romae, 1897), q. 89, art. VII, commentarium n. 12.

[34] *Theologia Moralis,* I, n. 167.

Reiffenstuel seemed to argue that the obligation of keeping such a forced oath arose simply from the positive law of the Church.[85] Finally, Schmalzgrueber, though holding the same strict opinion that such oaths were valid and rescissible only through competent authority, conceded that even an oath extorted by slight fear could be relaxed by a superior, since no injury was thereby caused to the one who compelled the taking of the oath. He referred to this doctrine as the common opinion.[86] The development of the doctrine regarding forced contracts and forced oaths which has been observed during this period contributed in a great measure to a clarification of the problems of imputability of forced actions and their consequent penalties.

Article IV. Imputability of Forced Acts

In the period of the *Corpus Iuris Canonici* the problem of imputability was treated only incidentally in the consideration of questions regarding forced contracts or oaths. This incidental treatment of the problem of imputability obtained also to some extent in Roman Law. But after the Council of Trent (1545-1563) canonists turned to a direct and thorough treatment of the question of imputability of forced acts. Here especially is seen the influence of Moral Theology on the doctrine of the canonists. Consequently the changes in this particular phase of the consideration of *vis* and *metus* are much more significant in this period than the changes respecting the treatment of contracts and oaths. In order to under-

85 " . . . cum frequenter juramentum interveniat in actibus hominum, aliter Ecclesia statuit circa ipsum, ne detur materia allegandi metum, sicque pejerandi, simulque ut habeatur in majori reverentia religio juramenti, probato metu debet peti absolutio ab eo."—lib. I, tit. XL, n. 59.

86 Lib. I, tit. XL, n. 23. Laymann (+1635) had also taught this before Schmalzgrueber: "Quae metu levi directe, et injuste incusso extorta sunt, aeque in foro conscientiae, et secundum legem naturae obnoxia sunt rescissioni, ac restitutioni . . . Quod vero in foro externo levem metum passo non conceditur id fit ob multitudinem litium vitandam: quemadmodum ob eandem causam decepto infra dimidium justi actio denegatur. Adde etiam in foro externo levem metum passo Judicis officio subveniri, si probetur, vel praesumi possit, effecisse consensum mixtum cum involuntario.—*Theologia Moralis*, lib. III, tract. IV, cap. VI, n. 4. For others holding this opinion cf. Schmalzgrueber, *loc. cit.*

stand the development in Moral Theology which played such a great rôle in the development of the canonical teaching of this period it is necessary to go back to the great Scholastics.

Alexander of Hales (+1245), conceding that the presence of external force excused from all guilt, taught that if there was only a question of fear, the agent was not excused entirely from fault, although at times he was excused from punishment. Referring to the words of Aristoltle, that some things are so wrong that they should never be done even under stress of fear,[37] he stated that, even though one is not excused from all guilt, one is then partly excused from the punishment since one is then burdened with a lesser guilt. This teaching later had an effect on the shaping of the doctrine on the incurring of penalties in the case of fear. Alexander expressly excluded *metus vanus* as an excuse from either guilt or punishment.[38]

The Carmelites of Salamanca (Salmanticenses 1665-1724) made a distinction between the formal and the material transgression of a law. Thus, although it diminished the guilt, fear did not excuse entirely in case of a formal transgression of the law. However, when fear was present the obligation of some laws ceased and hence there was only a material transgression and no consequent guilt. They held that human laws and even some divine laws did not bind unless they could be observed opportunely (*commode*), and that their obligation ceased when they could not be observed without danger of a grave evil. This interpretation, which became the common one among canonists and moralists of the 17th and later centuries, really sought to explore the problem of imputability in its fundamental phases.[39]

[37] *Nicomachean Ethics,* Book II, c. 1 (n. 1110a).

[38] *Summa Theologiae,* lib. III, inq. III, tract. VI, q. II, tit. I, c. VI. St. Bonaventure did not clearly admit fear as lessening culpability or as excusing from punishment when the matter was grievously sinful; cf. *Commentaria in Quatuor Libros,* lib. III *in Tertium Librum Sententiarum,* dist. XXXIX, art. III, q. II. St. Thomas seemed to hold the same view as St. Bonaventure on the influence of fear on culpability; cf. *Scriptum in Quartum Sententiarum,* dist. XXIX, art. I.

[39] *Cursus Theologicus Summam D. Thomae Complectens* (20 vols., Parisiis, Bruxellis, 1871-1885), Vol. V, tract. X, art. VI, n. 15 (hereafter

Among the earlier canonists Barbosa (1589-1649) had already taken cognizance of the teaching of Moral Theology that the laws of the Church do not ordinarily bind when grave fear is present. In commenting on canon 5 of the title *"De his quae vi metusve causa fiunt"* in the decretals of Gregory IX, he asserted that the communication with a major excummunicate in question there implied contempt of an ecclesiastical censure and consequently a sin against the natural and divine law.[40] Pirhing (+1679) stated explicitly that grave and just fear excused from the precepts and censures of the Church, because what was forbidden only by positive law was not so inherently evil that, if certain circumstances occurred, it did not cease to be evil and forbidden.[41] He even maintained that a grave matter concerning the public good, even when forbidden under censure, might sometimes be allowed if grave fear was present, because its observance was not always and in every instance so necessary to the public good that a grave offence or affront to ecclesiastical authority necessarily followed if such a grave matter was committed.[42]

cited *Cursus Theologicus)*: "Respondetur negando antecedens si intelligatur de transgressione formali legis [antecedens dicit metum gravem excusare a culpa]: existente enim huius obligatione, nullus metus excusat simpliciter a culpa; licet eam diminuat. Propterea vero non servans jejunium, vel non audiens Sacrum ob metum gravem non peccat, quia tunc cessat obligatio legis, eo quod leges humanae, et etiam aliquae divinae non obligant, nisi cum possunt commode observari; cum vero non possunt absque gravis mali periculo, cessat obligatio, et consequenter formalis earum transgressio. Actusque illi, vel omissiones materialiter dumtaxat dicentur contra legem, quatenus alias lege prohibeantur; non tamen hic et nunc ubi lex cessavit."

[40] Lib. I, tit. XL, ad c. 5; cf. also Sanchez (1150-1610), *Opus Morale in Praecepta Decalogi* (Parmae, 1723), lib. I, cap. 5, nn. 8, 9.

[41] Lib. I, tit. XL, n. 3; cf. also Laymann, *Theologia Moralis,* lib. I, tract, IV, cap. XIV, n. 5ss. tract. V, cap. V. n. 9.

[42] "Nec obstat, quod prohibitio sub censura sit res gravis concernens bonum publicum, adeoque obligat sub peccato gravi, non obstante quovis metu; nam non semper, et in omni casu est talis, ut ejus observantia sit necessaria ad commune bonum, vel, ut ex eo, quod non observetur, sequatur gravis offensio vel laesio auctoritatis Ecclesiae, ita ut fideles obligentur ad eam servandam, non obstante metu mortis. Et hinc etiam propter metum gravis infamiae, et jacturae gravis temporalium bonorum, excusatur quis, ne incurrat censuram, quia universim loquendo, leges positivae non obligant cum toto rigore, extra casus speciales."—*op. cit., loc. cit.*

Sporer (+1683) was perhaps the clearest of all the moralists of the 17th century in distinguishing the imputability of actions committed under grave fear. Asserting that fear of very grave evil could wholly excuse from sin indirectly, in so far as the law itself ceased to oblige in case of such evil or danger, he made the following distinctions which are the ones followed by practically all modern canonists and moral theologians. First, there were those acts which were intrinsically and objectively evil by being thus branded in the natural law itself, and hence could in no way become licit. Of such a character were lies, hatred of God, etc. No fear whatever could excuse from guilt in these actions, although grave fear could diminish guilt even in such acts. Secondly, grave fear excused even from the natural law in those things which could become licit, for the natural law ceased to bind in such cases. Thus the law against homicide ceased to bind when one's own life was threatened by an unjust aggressor. Thirdly, grave fear excused in the transgression of a positive divine law if it looked to the advantage or the utility of the one who placed the act. Such a law was the one regarding the integrity of confession. Finally, grave fear of death, etc., in and of itself always excused in the transgression of human laws or precepts, whether these were ecclesiastical or civil, for it was not considered to be the mind of the legislator that these laws should bind with such rigor, and in fact they could not thus bind, since otherwise they were not just and reasonable laws. He pointed out that dependently on incidental circumstances these latter laws could and did bind even in certain danger to life, fame or fortune, that is, whenever there intervened a superior law which was binding even in such danger. Hence these laws bound if contrariwise the common good would have suffered greatly, or if their violation would have entailed contempt for ecclesiastical authority, a denial of the Faith, harm to the Christian religion, the emergence of grave scandal, the spiritual ruin of one's neighbor, or the perpetration of sin in one's own life.[43]

[43] *Theologia Moralis,* lib. I, n. 161; cf. also Schmalzgrueber, lib. I, tit. XL, n. 7; Ferraris, *Bibliotheca,* s. v. *metus,* nn. 27, 28, 29; St. Alphonsus, *Theologia Moralis,* lib. I, n. 175. Wernz (+1914) added that even grave fear did not of itself take away the essence of a delict, although it did les-

Article V. Force and Fear in Relation to Penalties

I. Necessity of Grave Fault for Grave Punishment.

The first fundamental rule, common to pre-Code canonists in regard to all excuse from penalties, was the general maxim that whatever excused from grave fault excused also from grave punishment. This maxim was clearly founded upon the doctrine of the decretals. Rule 23 of the Rules of Law in the *Liber Sextus* states: "*Sine culpa, nisi subsit causa, non est aliquis puniendus,*" i.e., without any fault or with only slight fault, for the judge had no concern about a small matter like a slight fault.[44] This same rule was presupposed as applicable in all canonical discussions regarding force and fear as excuses.[45] Consequently, whenever fear sufficed to nullify the gravity of the sin it also precluded all grave punishment for the violation of the penal law.

It is to be noted, however, as Swoboda points out, that although the principle that no grave penalty could be imposed except for grave sin was universally admitted at least in theory, many authors held that a slight penalty could be imposed for venial guilt.[46] As examples of slight penalties the following were mentioned: minor excommunications,[47] *suspensio ab uno vel alio effectu non gravi ad*

sen the gravity of the delict. He explained this by maintaining that other canonists, such as Lega (1860-1935), confused fear and necessity. According to Wernz, necessity could co-exist with full voluntariness, but it exempted from the law since the law was not binding in such a case. Here the objective element was missing, namely, a law which had binding force, rather than the subjective element.—*Ius Decretalium,* VI, n. 19.

[44] Cf., e.g., c. 1, X, *de sententia excommunicationis,* V. 39; cap. un., *de homicidio voluntario vel casuali,* V, 4, in Clem.

[45] Cf. D'Annibale (1815-1892), *Summula Theologiae Moralis,* (5. ed., 3 vols., Romae, 1908) I, n. 312, note 69; St. Alphonsus, *Theologia Moralis,* lib. VII, nn. 31, 34; Suarez (1548-1617), *De Legibus et de Deo Legislatore—Opera Omnia* (Parisiis, 1856-1866), tom. V, cap. XII, n. 16.

[46] *Ignorance in Relation to the Imputability of Delicts.* The Catholic University of America Canon Law Studies, n. 143 (Washington, D. C.: The Catholic University of America Press, 1941), p. 72, n. 72 (hereafter cited *Ignorance).*

[47] Suarez, *De Censuris—Opera Omnia,* tom. XXIII, disp. IV, sect. IV, n. 6.

tempus breve,[48] *suspensio a Missa celebranda per unum vel alterum diem.*[49]

II. Fear as an Excuse in Ecclesiastical Laws

From the beginning of the post-Tridentine period the writers were explicit in excusing from all merely ecclesiastical laws in case of grave fear.[50] The authors pointed out that it was evident that no ecclesiastical penalty could be incurred if the law itself ceased to bind, and the erstwhile forbidden action was no longer sinful and forbidden.[51]

III. Fear as an Excuse in Divine Positive or Natural Law.

There was a dispute among pre-Code authors as to whether grave fear exempted from punishment if a sinful act was forbidden not merely by ecclesiastical but also by the divine positive or natural law. Many, especially among the early authors of this period, held that the obligation of the divine law did not cease in such instances, and that consequently there was no reason for the accompanying ecclesiastical law, i.e., the punishment connected with the law, to cease. Alexander of Hales (+1245) was usually considered to have held this view, but his words were not really clear on this subject. Thus he stated that grave fear, though not excusing in those things which were so evil that no fear should bring one to perform them, nevertheless partly excused from punishment even in such things.[52] The opinion which favored the non-cessation of the penal law under these circumstances was definitely held by Sanchez (1550-1610),[53]

[48] Passerinus (1595-1677), *Commentaria in Sextum Librum Decretalium* (Venetiis, 1698), lib. I, tit. II, cap. II, q. I, art. 21.

[49] Pirhing, lib. V, tit. XXXIX, sect. VI, n. 207; Reiffenstuel, *Theologia Moralis* (Mutinae, 1737), tract. XIII, dist. I, q. 2, n. 10.

[50] Cf. Barbosa, lib. I, tit. XL, ad c. 5; Pirhing, lib. I, tit. XL, n. 3; Sporer, *Theologia Moralis,* I, n. 161.

[51] Cf., e.g., Ojetti (1866-1933), *Synopsis Rerum Moralium et Iuris Pontificii* (3. ed., 4 vols., Romae, 1909-1914), s. v. *censura,* n. 965 (hereafter cited *Synopsis).*

[52] *Summa Theologiae,* lib. III, n. 50.

[53] *Opus Morale in Praecepta Decalogi,* tomus I, lib. I, c. XVIII, n. 4.

and was defended by Schmalzgrueber (1663-1736) as being the more probable opinion.[54]

The other opinion held that grave fear excused from punishment even in these cases. Already soon after the beginning of the present period Barbosa (1589-1649) referred to an opinion which was evidently a common one and which held that *culpa* alone was not sufficient for the incurring of a censure, but that *contumacia* had also to be present, which latter however was excluded by grave fear.[55] Suarez (1548-1617) clearly taught that if an ecclesiastical law prohibited under censure something forbidden by the divine law, e.g., incest, then fear could excuse from the censure, although not from the sin, for such a *voluntarium secundum quid* was not a sufficient basis for the existence of contumacy.[56]

Sporer held the opinion that whatever fear excused in whole or in part from guilt also excused from the punishment decreed for the delict. The reason he advanced was that contumacy and interpretative contempt were required for a censure, and that one who sinned only in consequence of grave fear, although he really sinned, could not be judged as contumacious or acting through contempt for ecclesiastical power, but rather through weakness.[57] Finally Ojetti (1866-1933) indicated the general rule that whatever excused from grave guilt excused also from grave censure, and that whatever excused from a delict or even only from contumacy, even though it did not excuse from a grave sin at times, excused from grave censures.[58]

These writers stressed the excuse from censure in this case without explicitly mentioning other grave ecclesiastical punishments. But St. Alphonsus (1696-1787) applied this opinion so as to excuse from all severe ecclesiastical punishments.[59] And contumacy, in so

[54] Lib. V, tit. XXXIX, n. 79.

[55] Lib. I, tit. XL, ad c. 5.

[56] *Summa,* (2 vols., Parisiis, 1858), lib. II, tract. XVIII, disp. IV, sect. III.

[57] *Theologia Moralis,* lib. I, n. 162. Cf. also Laymann, *Theologia Moralis,* lib. I, tract. V, cap. 5, n. 9.

[58] *Synopsis,* s. v. *censura,* n. 965.

[59] *Theologia Moralis,* lib. VII, n. 46.

far as it postulated the freedom of the will, was commonly regarded as a necessary condition for all grave ecclesiastical penalties.[60]

However, all authors admitted an exception to this last opinion, namely, when the observance of a law, even of a merely human law, was necessary for protecting the public good, or when its violation led to contempt of the faith, or of the law, or of the ecclesiastical authority. In such an instance the one who violated the law even through fear of death was not excused from the punishment attached to the law.[61]

IV. *Certain Law Requiring Special Subjective Imputability.*

1. In the Period Preceding the Constitution "*Apostolicae Sedis*" (1869).

Already in the period before the Council of Trent Panormitanus (1386-1453) had drawn attention to a distinction between those crimes which expressly or tacitly required a greater subjective imputability and those in relation to which any morally culpable transgression is sufficient to beget the incurring of the penalty.[62] Felinus Sandeus (1444-1503) made a similar distinction.[63]

During the present period this same distinction was commonly made between laws which expressly or tacitly postulated this *dolus* and those which envisaged no other requirement than a morally culpable transgression. Suarez (1548-1617), for instance, taught

[60] Cf. Crnica, "*De metu gravi ut causa eximente a poenis latae sententiae*",—*Jus Pontificium,* V (1925), 10.

[61] Cf., e.g., Reiffenstuel, lib. V. tit. XXXIX, n. 34; Laymann, *Theologia Moralis,* lib. I, tit. V, cap. 5, n. 9; Ballerini (1805-1881)—Palmieri (1829-1909), *Opus Theologicum Morale* (7 vols., Prati, 1889-1893), Vol. VII, n. 159; St. Alphonsus, *Theologia Moralis,* lib. VII, n. 46.

[62] *Commentaria in Quinque Libros Decretalium* ([5 vols. in 7, Venetiis, 1588] ad c. 2, X, *de constitutionibus,* I, 2): "Et hoc casu dic, quod si statutum, requirat dolum expressum, vel tacite, non habet locum in eo, qui fuit in lata culpa, licet pro modo culpa aliter sit puniendus." As examples of laws requiring this special imputability he cites, c. 29, C. XVII, q. 4, *(Si quis suadente diabolo)*—II General Lateran Council; c. 15, and c. 4, X, *de sententia excommunicationis,* V, 39.

[63] *Commentaria in Quinque Libros Decretalium* (2 vols., Venetiis, 1570) ad c. 2, X, *de constitutionibus,* I, 2, n. 4. Cf. Swoboda, *Ignorance,* pp. 52-53, 72-73.

that when the law contained such expressions as *qui praesumpserit hoc facere, qui temere hoc fecerit, etc.*, then a lessening of the freedom of the will excused from the punishment.[64]

However, it must be noted that in general canonists did not make a clear distinction between laws postulating perfect knowledge and freedom of the will (perfect *dolus*) and those which postulated simply the deliberate will to violate the law (simple *dolus*). The authors frequently interpreted the terms "*praesumpserit*, etc.", to mean merely that *dolus* was expressly postulated by the law which contained these terms, and that therefore a mere *culpa* or negligence did not suffice for the incurring of the penalty imposed by the law.[65] Moreover, since the problem of *dolus* dealt with the prerequisite of sufficient knowledge,[66] the authors often neglected to consider fear as a special excusing factor even when the terms "*praesumpserit, consulto*, etc.", were used in a law or statute.[67]

2. The Problem of *Dolus* and Perfect *Dolus* after the Constitution "*Apostolicae Sedis*."

The Constitution "*Apostolicae Sedis*" issued on October 12, 1869,[68] brought an important change in regard to the excuse from *latae sententiae* penalties. This Constitution substituted certain excommunications for those contained in the *Bulla* "*Coenae*," and added certain other *latae sententiae* penalties. The consideration of this Constitution is of particular importance in the present work because of the addition of a caution in the wording of certain censures regarding knowledge and deliberation. Here is found the evident use of the terms "*scienter, ausu temerario, praesumentes*, etc.", in the sense of perfect *dolus*. Thus this Constitution fixed the legal meaning of these terms in their present implication.[69]

64 *Summa*, lib. II, tract. XVIII, disp. IV, sect. III.

65 Cf. Swoboda, *Ignorance*, pp. 92-93.

66 Cf. Kuttner, *Schuldlehre*, pp. 74-76.

67 Thus, e.g., St. Alphonsus, *Theologia Moralis*, lib. VII, nn. 45-47; D'Annibale, *Summula Theologiae Moralis*, I, n. 312.

68 *Fontes*, n. 552.

69 Cf. Hollweck, *Die Kirchlichen Strafgesetze* (Mainz, 1899), pp. 96-97, § 29, note 3.

It should be noted that Pius IX (1846-1878) here directed his attention almost exclusively to "censures" incurred *ipso facto ipsoque iure.* Hence his Constitution furnishes no explicit norm for *ferendae sententiae* penalties or for penalties inflicted *ab homine.*[70] And although it is true that most of the authors continued to consider only the requisite of full knowledge when commenting upon these terms,[71] some took cognizance of the requisite of full liberty in all delicts with reference to which these terms were used. Consequently they affirmed that fear excused from *latae sententiae* penalties if the law contained these terms.[72]

None of the pre-Code authors went into an explicit treatment of the question whether fear excused in those delicts which postulated perfect *dolus* if the delict led to contempt of the faith, etc. Although the question seems to be answered in the affirmative by the Constitution *Apostolicae Sedis,* it was left to the Code of Canon Law and the commentators on the Code to settle definitely this important question of penal responsibility.

Conclusion

Despite the relative lack of positive ecclesiastical legislation in this matter, the present period was most productive in determining the influence of force and fear in the various spheres of Canon Law. Thus the current common opinion regarding the voidability of ordinary contracts and the nullity of certain types of contracts became

[70] Cf. Leech, *A Comparative Study of the Constitution "Apostolicae Sedis" and the "Codex Iuris Canonici",* The Catholic University of America Canon Law Studies, n. 15 (Washington, D. C., 1922), pp. 10-11.

[71] Cf., e.g., Aichner (1816-1911), *Compendium Iuris Ecclesiastici* (9. ed., Brixinae, 1900), p. 768; Wernz, *Ius Decretalium,* VI, n. 158; De Brabandere (1828-1895)—De Meester, *Iuris Canonici Compendium* (Brugis, 1916), III n. 1376. Cf. also Claeys Bouuaert, *"De metus influxu quoad valorem actuum et quoad delicta et poenas secundum Codicem Juris Canonici,"—Jus Pontificium,* VI (1926), 141.

[72] Cf., e.g., Santi (1830-1885)—Leitner (1862-1929), *Praelectiones Juris Canonici* (4 ed., 5 vols. in 2, Ratisbonae, 1903-1905), tom. II, vol. V, p. 192, n. 13.

the law now adopted in the Code.[73] The question of the forced oath, which was decided in much the same manner as in the period immediately preceding the Council of Trent, is also so determined in the present law.[74]

Finally the greatest progress in this period is seen in the explicit treatment of the specific problem in question here, namely, the question of the imputability of forced acts and of the relation of such acts to ecclesiastical punishments. That the conclusions arrived at and the principles set down in this period by both moralists and canonists were substantially the same as they are now found in present day legislation will be pointed out in the commentary section which follows.

Thus the application of the ethical principles of Aristotle—which had entered through the Scholastics—to the Roman Law concepts as introduced at the time of Alexander III (1159-1181) helped to shape the present day law in regard to the imputability of acts performed through force or fear, and in regard to the liability for legal punishments in such cases.

[73] "Actus positi ex metu gravi et iniuste incusso vel ex dolo, valent, nisi aliud iure caveatur; sed possunt ad normam can. 1684-1689 per iudicis sententiam rescindi, sive ad petitionem partis laesae sive ex officio."—canon 103, § 2. Cf. also cc. 1684-1689; 169; 185; 542; 1°; 572 § 1, 4°; 1087; 1095, § 1, 3°; 1307, § 3; 2238.

[74] Iusiurandum per vim aut metum gravem extortum valet, sed a Superiore ecclesiastico relaxari potest."—canon 1317, § 2.

PART II

CANONICAL COMMENTARY

CHAPTER III

IMPUTABILITY OF CRIME

Article I. The Elements of a Delict

The consideration of the rôle of force and fear in determining delictual imputability and penal responsibility can best be approached by considering the essential elements of crime in general. In considering these elements one must pay special notice to the subjective element, namely imputability in particular.

According to the Code, a delict is an external and morally imputable violation of a law to which is attached some canonical sanction, at least an indeterminate one.[1] This definition gives the three essential elements of every crime. They are: the objective element, namely, the actual external violation of the law; the juridical element, that is the canonical sanction; and, finally, the subjective element, or imputability in particular.[2]

The first element to be considered in a delict is the objective, material element, the actual violation of the law, which inflicts the particular injury upon the social order. This element is referred to in canon 2195, § 1 as *"externa legis violatio."*[3] This

[1] Canon 2195, § 1.

[2] A detailed study of this subject will be found in Wernz-Vidal, *Ius Canonicum* (7 vols., in 8, Romae: Universitas Gregoriana, 1923-1938) VII, *Ius Poenale Ecclesiasticum,* 29-34; Roberti, *De Delictis et Poenis* (edito altera, Vol. I, Romae: Libraria Pontificii Instituti Utriusque Iuris, 1938), I, 53-55; Michiels, *De Delictis et Poenis* (Vol I, Lublin: Universitas Catholica, 1934), I, De Delictis, 56-59; Latini, *Iuris Criminalis Philosophici Summa Lineamenta* (Romae: Marietti, 1924), pp. 67-71 (hereafter cited *Lineamenta).* Cf. also Swoboda, *Ignorance,* pp. 82-84.

[3] According to canon 2195, § 2, the violation of a precept has generally the same effects as that of a law. The law in question may also be either universal or particular. In the present work, unless otherwise stated, what is said of law in general applies also to a particular statute or precept.

objective element is the first to be considered, since it forms the basis or foundation of every question regarding penalties. There can be no question of just penalties apart from such a violation, for if there be no violation there is no necessity of restoring the social and juridical order, no injury of the law to be corrected.

The quality or specific malice of a delict is to be judged from the object of the law.[4] And the nature of the law violated together with the damage done and the degree of subjective imputability determines also the quantity of the delict.[5] Hence in the application of a canonical penalty the nature of the law is the first measure or standard to be applied.[6] A delict is ordinarily the violation of an ecclesiastical law. However, the Church punishes also the violation of a divine law if it redounds to the detriment of ecclesiastical society;[7] otherwise the punishment is left entirely to God Himself.[8]

The Church, being an external visible society, is concerned in her penal legislation mainly with crimes against the social order. In order to constitute such an injury the violation of a law must be external.[9] Yet the legislator does not consider all external transgressions of the moral or ethical order as crimes, but only such that as a matter of public policy are considered to constitute a danger or *damnum* to the social order. The purpose of ecclesiastical penal laws is to prevent the disturbance of this external social order, and, when prevention has proved fruitless, to reinstate and restore the social order.[10]

The second essential element of a delict is called the juridical or social element. This consists in the penal sanction or penalty

[4] Canon 2196.

[5] Canon 2196.

[6] Canon 2218, § 1.

[7] E.g., the *ferendae sententiae* penalties against blasphemy and perjury,—canon 2323.

[8] Ayrinhac, H. A., and Lydon, P. J., *Penal Legislation in the New Code of Canon Law,* (revised edition, New York: Benziger, 1936) p. 2 (here after cited: *Penal Legislation);* Michiels, De Delictis et Poenis, 1, 63.

[9] "Cogitationis poenam nemo patitur."—c. 14, D. I, de poenit.; D. (48. 19) 18.

[10] Cf. Swoboda, *Ignorance,* p. 83.

placed by the lawgiver or commanding authority upon the violation of the law.[11] Thus the Code in practice adopts the axiom of "No crime, no punishment, without a previous penal law." But this is not to be understood in the sense that the penal sanctions must be always specifically determined. Although at times so determined, at other times it is merely a general indeterminate threat of punishment. And in consideration of canon 2222, § 1, it is considered sufficient that the law empower the proper authority to inflict a penalty in some specific instances.[12]

The third essential element of a delict, namely imputability in particular, is of especial importance in the present work and hence requires a more detailed treatment. The following article will discuss this, the subjective element in a delict.

Article II. Imputability in Particular

The subjective element essential to every delict is indicated in canon 2195, § 1, in the words: " . . . *moraliter imputabilis legis violatio*." Not every harmful action injuring the social order can be justly punished. Such an action must be also morally culpable or morally imputable. In other words, the law punishes with canonical sanctions only those acts which proceed from a free human agent, and, moreover, only in so far as these acts arise from a free principle and can be attributed to the latter as their author and master. The reason for this is evident. The juridic-social order does not constitute an order by itself, separated from and, as it were, parallel to the moral order. It is an integral part of the whole moral order constituted by God and also binding in conscience. Hence it is said to be subordinated to the general principles of the moral order. Now, since according to the fundamental principles of human reason the moral order cannot be injured except by acts morally imputable to the agent, so also the juridic-social order, which is a constitutive part of the moral order, cannot be injured except by external acts morally imputable to the agent.[13]

[11] Canon 2195, § 1.

[12] Cf. Swoboda, *Ignorance*, p. 84; Michiels, *De Delictis et Poenis*, I, 78-82.

[13] Cf. Michiels, *De Delictis et Poenis*, I, 98-99.

As the authors point out, the Code uses no uniform technical expression to denote this element of a delict.[14] The usual term is *imputabilitas.*[15] The term is evidently technical in this connection.[16] However, the term "*culpa*"[17] and its derived forms *culpabilitas*[18] and *culpabilis*[19] are also frequently used to connote imputability in general.[20] *Culpa* also has a particular technical meaning,[21] which will be discussed later.

In the present work the term "imputability" will be used to denote this third essential element of a delict, the subjective element in general, and *culpa* and *dolus* will be used only in their specific and technical meaning according to canon 2199.

I. The Nature of Imputability[22]

The word *imputare* (from *in* and *putare*—to reckon or compute) means to bring into reckoning, to charge.[23] Imputability is thus the necessary moral condition for a judgment by which in the abstract some good or bad act is attributed to an individual. Imputation, on the other hand, is the judgment by which some good or bad act is actually ascribed to a certain person in the concrete.

[14] Cf. Moersdorf, *Die Rechtssprache des Codex Juris Canonici* (Paderborn: Schöningh, 1937), p. 372; Swoboda, *Ignorance,* p. 84.

[15] Canons 2196; 2197, 4°; 2199; 2201, § 4; 2202, §§ 1, 2; 2204; 2205, §§ 3, 4; 2206; 2209, §§ 3, 4, 5, 6, 7; 2213, §§ 1, 3.

[16] Cf. the inscription of Title II: *De imputabilitate delicti, de causis illam aggravantibus vel minuentibus et de iuridicis delicti effectibus;* canon 2199.

[17] Cf. canons 829; 1455, 2°; 1476, § 2; 1644, § 3; 1737; 1553, § 1, 2°; 2193; 2322, 1°; 2324; 2325, 2331, § 1.

[18] Cf. canons 2208, § 2; 2209, §§ 1, 5.

[19] Cf. canons 2209, § 2; 2213, § 2; 2184; 2354, § 2.

[20] Some authors employ the term *dolus* to designate imputability in general. This term, as Swoboda notes *(Ignorance,* p. 84, note 17) should be reserved for a very special form or degree of imputability, as will be shown later.

[21] Canon 2199.

[22] Cf. Wernz-Vidal, *Ius Canonicum,* VIII, 39-40; Roberti, *De Delictis et Poenis,* I, 86-87; Michiels, *De Delictis et Poenis,* I, 82-100; Swoboda, *Ignorance,* pp. 85-88.

[23] Cf. *Harper's Latin Dictionary* (ed. Lewis and Short, Oxford: Clarendon Press, 1882) s. v. *imputo.*

One can distinguish physical and moral imputability. Physical imputability can be spoken of in the sense that an effect is ascribed to a physical agent as to its efficient cause. In this sense, for example, light and heat are 'imputable' to fire. Moral imputability is had when the effect of some action or omission comes from a free voluntary cause. In this sense imputability is called "a moral proprietorship in the praise or blame justly due to deliberate acts performed by a free agent." [24] The moral imputability is that which is mentioned in canon 2195, § 1. But canons 2199-2213 deal with another form of imputability, which presupposes moral imputability but is distinct from it. This is termed juridical or political imputability.[25]

Juridico-criminal imputability is defined as a property of an anti-juridic act whereby this act is subjected to the penal power of society. Now this juridical imputability, as stated above, presupposes moral imputability, for the Church does and can punish only those acts over which a man is master, over which he exercises true dominion.[26] It was also mentioned that juridico-criminal imputability differs from moral imputability. The principles of moral imputability are derived from reason, are philosophical or ethical. But the rules governing juridical imputability are dictated by public policy to meet certain social needs, and consequently need not always be perfectly logical. Some of these rules are, from

[24] Augustine, *A Commentary on the New Code of Canon Law* (8 vols., Vol. VIII, *Penal Code)* (St. Louis: Herder, 1922) VIII, 22.

[25] Roberti *(De Delictis et Poenis,* I, 87) distinguishes between political and juridical imputability. According to him, the former is determined by the legislator when he states that the author of certain acts must be held responsible to society, while juridical imputability is determined by the magistrate when he in a concrete case decides that the author of a crime must be held accountable. The authors, however, generally use the two terms in the same significance. Cf. Swoboda, *Ignorance,* p. 86, note 21; Coronata, *Institutiones Iuris Canonici* (5 vols., Vols. I-II, 2 ed., 1938; Vols. III-V, 1933-1936, Taurini: Marietti) IV, 8; Michiels, *De Delictis et Poenis,* I, 98-100.

[26] "Quorum igitur nos sumus domini, eorum principia extrinsecus non requiramus . . . sed agnoscamus ea, quae proprie nostra sunt."—c. 6, C. XV, q. 1.

a rational point of view, more or less arbitrary, as, for example, the presumptions of the external forum.[27]

II. Imputability and Responsibility

For a correct understanding of the penal law of the Code and of certain divisions of the Fifth Book it is necessary to distinguish clearly imputability and responsibility. As noted above, imputability denotes a particular relationship of moral causality between an agent and his act. This is distinct from responsibility. The latter indicates a relationship between the agent and some third party.[28] In the field of penal law a crime is imputable to a delinquent, but the delinquent is responsible to society. Here responsibility means that the delinquent is answerable to society and must, therefore, pay the penalty imposed by law. It is the opposite of excuse from penalty.[29]

A realization of the distinction between responsibility and imputability is of great importance in considering excuse from penalties. It is only by keeping this distinction in mind that one can fully understand the purpose of Title II, Part I, as distinct from that of Title VI, Part II, of the Fifth Book. For responsibility and imputability are not only distinct and different concepts, referring to essentially different relationships, but they need not always be present together at the same time in a concrete case.

Canon 2228 presupposes a distinction between the imputability of a delict and the responsibility for a determined penalty. This canon ordains that the penalty determined by law is not incurred unless the crime be perfectly consummated according to the strict wording of the law. This is well illustrated by a comparison of the two canons of especial importance in this study. According to canon 2205, § 3, certain crimes such as those which involve acts intrinsically evil may be imputable to delinquents acting even through grave fear, while in canon 2229, §§ 2, 3, these same delinquents are excused from specific *latae sententiae* penalties and

[27] Canons 2200, § 2; 2201, § 2; 2204. Cf. Swoboda, *Ignorance*, p. 86.

[28] Roberti (*De Delictis et Poenis*, I, 87) gives the example of the creation of the world. He notes that this is imputable to God, but He is responsible to no one.

[29] Swoboda, *Ignorance*, p. 87.

hence are not responsible for these determined punishments.[80] This same distinction is also evident from canon 2242, § 1, in which the elements of a crime punishable with censure are described. Here the legislator requires an especially aggravating circumstance, namely *contumacia,* before the delinquent can be held responsible with respect to the incurring of the punishment of a censure.[81]

III. The Elements of Imputability

The notion of imputability includes two elements, namely, deliberation and free will. Knowledge is a prerequisite for every act imputable as deliberate, and at least the possibility of knowledge is required for criminal negligence. At times the law lays particular stress upon this element in using terms such as *deliberatio,*[82] *scienter,*[83] and the like.[84]

The second element, free will, is really the cause of the crime, for the crime is formally constituted by the will. This important rôle of the free will is emphasized in the terminology of those texts in which the subjective element or imputability is called *animus*[85] or *voluntas,*[86] or is qualified by the word *sponte.*[87]

The question of the diminution or execution of imputability on the part of the will is of concern in the present study. Of the various defects of freedom only such a defect as is caused by force or fear, and to some extent also that which is caused by the closely allied factors of necessity and hardship, will be considered here.

[80] Cf. Michiels, *De Delictis et Poenis,* I, 113.

[81] Cf. also canons 2229, § 4; 2230; 2233, § 2; 2242.

[82] Cf. e.g., canons 2200, § 1; 2206; 2229, § 2.

[83] Cf. e.g., canons 1755, § 3; 2316; 2319, § 1, 3° and 4°; 2326; 2338, §§ 2, 3.

[84] Swoboda, *Ignorance,* p. 88.

[85] C. 45, D. L; *animus simoniacus*—canon 728; *animus malitiosus*—canon 644, § 2.

[86] C. 46, D. L; " . . . crimen enim contrahitur, si et voluntas nocendi intercedit,"—c. 47, D. L; *perversa voluntas*—canon 657; *studiosa voluntas*—canon 727, § 1; *mala voluntas*—canon 2185; *deliberata voluntas*—canon 2200, § 1.

[87] " . . . si clericus alicui sponte duellum obtulerit . . . "—c. 1, X, *de clericis pugnantibus in duello,* V, 14; canons 2339; 2390, § 2. For further references cf. Swoboda, *Ignorance,* p. 88, notes 30-32.

IV. Degrees of Imputability

The Code speaks of two degrees of imputability, *dolus* and *culpa.*[38] The division of imputability corresponds in a general way to the distinction of the *voluntarium* into the *voluntarium directum* and the *voluntarium indirectum.*[39] This division is of importance, since according to canons 2196 and 2218, § 1, the quantity or gravity of a crime and the consequent severity of the penalty depend not only on the gravity of the law violated and the damage inflicted but also upon the subjective guilt of the agent. This subjective guilt in turn varies in each concrete case according to the circumstances which affect the intensity of the anti-juridical will and the consciousness and the knowledge of the delinquent. Thus the degree of imputability and of responsibility will depend on the degree of subjective malice or of culpability in ignorance or neglect.[40]

1. *Dolus*

"*. . . deliberata voluntas violandi legem.*"[41]

Dolus is defined as the deliberate will to violate the law. This is the technical definition of *dolus* as given in the Fifth Book of the Code. Hence a *delictum dolosum* is a crime committed with the deliberate will to violate the law.[42] According to the definition, two things are necessary for *dolus* or a *delictum dolosum:* the will to violate the law and deliberation in the act of violating it. Re-

[38] "Imputabilitas delicti pendet ex dolo . . . vel ex . . . culpa . . . "—canon 2199.

[39] Cf. Michiels, *De Delictis et Poenis,* I, 101.

[40] Cf. Ayrinhac-Lydon, *Penal Legislation,* p. 6.

[41] Canon 2200, § 1.

[42] The term *dolus* has a variety of meanings in legal language. Both in Roman and Canon Law the term has several meanings. The Code uses *dolus* in the Roman Law meaning of cunning, deceit, and deliberate deception, i.e., outside of penal legislation. Cf. Bieter, "The Canon Law on Deceit"—*ER,* LVI (1922), 42-51; canons 48, § 2; 52; "Actus positi . . . ex dolo, valent, nisi aliud iure caveatur."—canon 103, § 2; canons 169, § 1, 1°; 185; 572, § 1, 4°. Even in penal laws the term does not always retain its technical meaning. Thus canon 2387 uses the term in defining the crime of a religious who has deliberately and deceitfully entered into an invalid profession. Cf. also canons 2353; 2361; Swoboda, *Ignorance,* pp. 89-90.

garding the latter, suffice it to note that there must be knowledge of the law against which the delinquent offends. And this knowledge must be had at a time when it can be said to be at least morally connected with the action.[43]

As regards the will to violate the law, it should be noted that this condition does not imply a direct intention to commit a crime. It is sufficient that the action be actually willed, provided that one have knowledge that the same is prohibited. It is important to keep this in mind when considering the rôle of fear as an excuse from imputability and responsibility.

Of particular interest in any treatment of the problem of penal responsibility is the distinction between simple *dolus* and perfect *dolus*. This distinction is of importance in understanding the legal principles regarding the effects of fear upon responsibility, and a proper knowledge of this distinction is especially necessary for the practical application of these principles to individual laws.[44] Even after the Code there has been no little discussion among the authors as to this distinction and its application to the individual penal laws. Consequently, it is necessary to give attention to these various points in a study like the present one.

A. The Existence and the Nature of the Distinction Between Simple *Dolus* and Perfect *Dolus*

The pre-Code canonists, especially those who wrote before the Constitution *Apostolicae Sedis* (1869), paid comparatively little attention to this distinction of simple *dolus* and perfect *dolus*. The distinction gradually evolved in the doctrine of the canonists concerning the excuse occasioned by grave fear and particularly by crass and supine ignorance relative to the incurring of censures.[45]

Although canonists generally made the distinction between penal laws which incorporated such terms as "*praesumpserit, scienter, consulto egerit*" and the laws which did not incorporate such

[43] Cf. Swoboda, *Ignorance,* pp. 90-91.

[44] Canonists give various other divisions of *dolus,* which need not be considered here. Cf. Michiels, *De Delictis et Poenis,* I, 103-105; Roberti, *De Delictis et Poenis,* I, 90-91.

[45] Cf. *supra,* p. 50, Swoboda, *Ignorance,* pp. 72-74.

terms,[46] they frequently interpreted these terms to mean merely that *dolus* was expressly required, and consequently that *lata culpa* did not suffice for the penalty imposed by the law. It seems that most of the canonists did not draw a clear distinction between *dolus* in general and the *dolus* postulated in these laws.[47] But some authors did point out that the laws which contained these expressions did presuppose a *voluntarium directum* and *perfectum* in the question of their violation if the enacted penalties were to be applicable.[48]

The Code itself has adopted the doctrine or theory proposed in its substance by Hollweck (1854-1926). He distinguished *dolus* in the strict sense *(Vorsätzlichkeit)* and *dolus* in a broad sense *(Freiwilligkeit)*. In the strict sense *dolus* implied a greater degree of freedom and a stronger adherence of the will to the forbidden object. *Dolus* in the broad sense *(voluntas* and *voluntarie* in the sources) connoted a more positive use of freedom than did *culpa*, but it did not necessarily imply any higher degree of guilt.[49]

The terms, now considered technical terms which postulate perfect freedom of the will, originally, that is, when the laws were actually written, had no special meaning attached to them. This is shown by a study of the actual use of these terms. Hollweck clearly pointed out that until the Constitution *Apostolicae Sedis*

[46] Cf. Suarez (1548-1617), *De Censuris*, disp. IV, sect. X, nn. 2-3; Sanchez (1550-1610), *De Sancto Matrimonii Sacramento* (3 vols. in 2, Antverpiae, 1607) lib. IX, disp. XXXII, nn. 35-38 (hereafter cited *De Matrimonio)*; Lehmkuhl (1834-1914), *Theologia Moralis* (5. ed., 2 vols., Friburgi Brisgoviae, 1888) II, 621; Wernz, *Ius Decretalium*, VI, 31, note 79.

[47] Cf. e.g., Sanchez, *De Matrimonio*, lib. XI, disp. XXXII, n. 35; after the Code, Sipos, *Enchiridion Iuris Canonici* (2.ed., Pécs: "Haladas R. T.", 1931), p. 109 (hereafter cited *Enchiridion)*; Eichmann, *Lehrbuch des Kirchenrechts auf Grund des Codex Iuris Canonici* (2. ed., Paderborn, Schöningh, 1926), 670 (hereafter cited *Lehrbuch des Kirchenrechts)*.

[48] Konings (1821-1884), *Theologia Moralis* (4. ed., 2 vols., New York, 1880), II, 311; Gury (1801-1866), Ballerini (1805-1881), *Compendium Theologiae Moralis* (3. ed., 2 vols., Romae, 1874-1875), II, 934.

[49] *Die kirchlichen Strafgesetze*, p. 75, § 13, note 5.

of Pius IX (1869) [50] these terms had no fixed legal meaning.[51]

These terms seem to have referred rather to the objective gravity of the crime than to the special degree of subjective imputability postulated for the incurring of the threatened penalty. This is shown, as Swoboda notes,[52] in the fact that these terms were often employed to add solemnity to the decree or canon for the sake of stressing the gravity of the crime. Hence one sees the terms used frequently in connection with such crimes as heresy, simony, the abuse or usurpation of authority, the violation of or disregard for an ecclesiastical penalty, or the violation of the *privilegium canonis.*[53]

Since these words did not always have the specific meaning which is given them at the present time, their use in former legislation cannot be appealed to in order to establish that a special degree of *dolus* is required in some doubtful case in the Code. The application of this negative rule obtained for the time prior to the issuance of the Constitution *Apostolicae Sedis* (1869).[54] However, these terms did occasion the interpretation which must now be given to them. It was this interpretation of individual laws which was adopted by the Code. Therefore the writings and opinions of the canonists of those times are not only a safe guide to pre-Code interpretation of pre-Code statutory use of these terms but also of their use in the Code.

The Code itself is quite clear in distinguishing between *dolus* in general and the special degree of *dolus* postulated in such terms as "*praesumpserit, ausus fuerit, consulto egerit,*" and the like. *Dolus* in general is defined in canon 2200, § 1, as the "deliberate will to violate the law." Canon 2229, § 2 speaks of a *dolus* in which full knowledge and complete deliberation is necessary. This kind of *dolus* is precluded by any diminution of that fulness and com-

[50] *Fontes,* n. 552.

[51] *Die kirchlichen Strafgesetze,* pp. 96-97, § 29, note 3. A number of these terms had already been employed by the decretists to express criminal intent, or what we refer to as *dolus* in general.

[52] *Ignorance,* p. 95.

[53] For numerous examples of such a use of the terms cf. Swoboda, *Ignorance,* p. 95, notes 59-63.

[54] *Fontes,* n. 552.

pleteness of activity on the part either of the intellect or of the will.

Since the Code, canonists generally make this same distinction. But they use a variety of terms to express the special degree of *dolus* which is presupposed in the laws which contain the words *praesumpserit, ausus fuerit,* etc. Some of the terms used are, v. g., "special *dolus*",[55] "perfect and full *dolus*"[56] "*dolus plenissimus*",[57] or "full and perfect responsibility".[58] The term used most frequently by canonists is "perfect *dolus*".[59] It will also be employed in the present study since it is sufficiently accurate.

B. Penal Laws Postulating Perfect *Dolus*

In order to understand the rôle of force and fear as causes excusing from penal responsibility in a specific case it is necessary to know which penal laws postulate perfect *dolus* and which postulate only simple *dolus.* First to be considered are those which postulate perfect *dolus.*[60] Canon 2229, § 2, expressly enumerates certain terms which indicate when perfect *dolus* is postulated. Of these, the term "*praesumpserit*" appears nineteen times in the various canons.[61] "*Ausus fuerit*" is found six times,[62] *scienter* eighteen times.[63] The other three terms, namely "*studiose, temerarie, con-*

[55] Vermeersch-Creusen, *Epitome Iuris Canonici* (Vol. I, 6. ed., 1937; Vols. II-III, 5. ed., 1934-1936, Mechlinae: H. Dessain), III, 209 (hereafter cited *Epitome).*

[56] Wernz-Vidal, *Ius Canonicum,* VII, 214.

[57] Vermeersch-Creusen, *Epitome,* III, 248; Sipos *(Enchiridion,* p. 934) calls it simply *dolus plenus.*

[58] Berutti, *Institutiones Iuris Canonici,* VI, *De Delictis et Poenis* (Taurini-Romae: Marietti, 1938), p. 91.

[59] Roberti, *De Delictis et Poenis,* I, 276; Swoboda, *Ignorance,* p. 92.

[60] Cf. Moersdorf, *Die Rechtssprache des Codex Iuris Canonici,* p. 374; Swoboda, *Ignorance,* pp. 97-98.

[61] Canons 1625, § 2, 1755, § 3; 2321; 2338, § 1; 2346; 2347; 2365; 2366; 2369, § 1; 2372; 2388; 2390, § 2; 2393, 2396, 2399, 2400, 2406, § 1, 2410, 2412, 1°.

[62] Canons 2337; § 1; 2339; 2341; 2364; 2365; 2375.

[63] Canons 1755, § 3; 2316; 2318, § 1; 2319, § 1, 3°, 4°; 2326; 2338, §§ 2, 3; 2347, 3°; 2360, § 1; 2362; 2368, § 2; 2371; 2390, § 2; 2391, §§ 1, 2, 3; 2395.

sulto", though often found in the sources, are not found in that precise form in the present Code. A modified form of *temerarie,* namely *temere* is used in canon 2369, § 2. That this term postulates perfect *dolus* is evident from its connection with *temerarie* and the content of canon 2369.[64] *Studiose* can be considered as implied in canons 2371 and 2392 which deal with simony. The definition of this crime in canon 727 shows that simony presupposes a *studiosa voluntas.*[65]

The authors generally enumerate four other terms as similar expressions which postulate perfect *dolus,* namely,*pertinaciter,*[66] *malitiose,*[67] *fraude et dolo,*[68] and *de industria.*[69] Roberti, though noting that *de industria* and *fraude et dolo* in themselves seem to postulate only *dolus,* admits that of itself *consulto* likewise would

[64] This same term is used also in canons 1625, § 1 and 1910, § 2. *Temerarius* is used in canon 1915, § 1. However, the context of these canons shows that the word *temere* or *temerarius* connotes merely rashness, or as Noval interprets it, acting "without any reasonable foundation."—*Commentarium Codicis Iuris Canonici,* Libr. IV, *De Processibus,* Pars. I, *De Iudiciis* (Augustae Taurinorum: Marietti, 1920), n. 217 (hereafter cited *De Processibus,* I).

It is to be noted that the terms mentioned in canon 2229, § 2 are the same as those enumerated by Wernz, except that he mentioned *temere* instead of *temerarie.*—*Ius Decretalium,* VI, 31, note 79.

[65] "Studiosa voluntas emendi vel vendendi pro pretio temporali rem intrinsece spiritualem . . . vel rem temporalem rei spirituali adnexam ita ut res temporalis sine spirituali nullo modo esse possit . . . aut res spiritualis sit obiectum, etsi partiale, contractus . . . est simonia iuris divini."—canon 727, § 1.

[66] Found in canons 2317 and 2331; it is also implied in canon 2314 in regard to the crime of heresy by reason of the definition given in canon 1325, § 2.

[67] As it is used in canon 2374. Swoboda (*Ignorance,* p. 99, note 76) points out that it is not used in this sense in canon 2354, § 1.

[68] Canon 2361 uses the expression "*fraude vel dolo*". However, the context shows that the meaning here is rather "fraud or deceit."

[69] Found in canon 2351. Cf. Beste, *Introductio in Codicem* (Collegeville, Minn.: St. John's Abbey Press, 1938), p. 894; Chelodi, *Ius Poenale et Ordo Procedendi in Iudiciis Criminalibus* (1. ed., [Tridenti: Libr. Edit. Tridentum, 1920] reprinted, Tridenti, 1925) p. 31, note 5 (hereafter cited *Ius Poenale);* Michiels, *Normae Generales* (2 vols., Lublin: Universitas Catholica, 1929), I, 359; Wernz-Vidal, *Ius Canonicum,* II, 214.

seem to postulate only *dolus*. But since *consulto* is mentioned in the Code explicitly as postulating perfect *dolus*, it can safely be admitted that these two phrases also postulate perfect *dolus*.[70] External authority also indicates that such an interpretation is solidly probable.[71]

C. Canons Presupposing *Dolus* to the Exclusion of a *Delictum Culposum*

Some delicts, while not postulating perfect *dolus*, do of their very nature or by the express will of the legislator presuppose *dolus* to the exclusion of a mere *delictum culposum*. This can be seen in the very definition of some delicts. These postulate a direct will *(voluntarium directum)* to commit the action, and hence cannot take place through mere negligence.[72] Here are included the *procurantes abortum*,[73] the *attentantes* of a civil marriage,[74] the *fabricatores* and *falsarii* of papal rescripts and other ecclesiastical documents,[75] the electors who are *sollicitantes immixtionem* of lay power in a canonical election,[76] and the *iniicientes violentas manus* in violation of the *privilegium canonis*. Regarding the latter, be it noted that *dolus* is postulated for this delict because the very concept of an *iniuriosa violatio* presupposes *dolus*. Hence the fact that the Code in canon 2343 no longer has the phrase *"si quis suadente diabolo"* implies no change in the principle formulated by the decretists: *"Violentia sine dolo non committitur"*.[77]

[70] *De Delictis et Poenis*, I, 277.

[71] Cf. Chelodi, *Ius Poenale*, p. 30, note 1; Beste, *Introductio in Codicem*, p. 894; Swoboda, *Ignorance*, p. 99.

[72] Cf. Swoboda, *Ignorance*, p. 100.

[73] Canon 2350. Cf. Cappello, *De Censuris iuxta Codicem Iuris Canonici* (3. ed., Taurinorum Augustae: Marietti, 1933) p. 334 (hereafter cited *De Censuris)*; Cerato, *Censurae Vigentes Ipso Facto a Codice Iuris Canonici Excerptae* (2. ed., Patavii: Typis Seminarii, 1921), pp. 99-100 (hereafter cited *Censurae Vigentes)*; Vermeersch-Creusen, *Epitome* III, n. 551; Ayrinhac-Lydon, *Penal Legislation*, pp. 242-243.

[74] Canon 2356. Cf. Coronata, *Institutiones Iuris Canonici*, IV, 489.

[75] Canons 2360; 2362. Cf. Ayrinhac-Lydon, *Penal Legislation*, p. 258; Vermeersch-Creusen, *Epitome*, III, n. 562; Cappello, *De Censuris*, p. 255.

[76] Canon 2390, § 2.

[77] Swoboda, *Ignorance*, pp. 100-101; D'Annibale, *In Constitutionem Apostolicae Sedis Commentarii* (5. ed., 3 vols., Romae, 1909), p. 74; Eich-

There are three other terms which seem to presuppose *dolus,* namely *usurpare,*[78] *conspirare,*[79] and *dolose detrectare.*[80] For, as Swoboda points out,[81] it is hard to understand how one could become guilty of the delicts described and defined by these terms through mere negligence or *culpa.*

The word *sponte* is used alone in canons 2390, § 2, and 2339. Swoboda maintains that this term indicates merely that simple *dolus* is postulated. He argues from the presence of *scienter* in the canons where the Code evidently requires perfect *dolus,* from pre-Code usage in which it is employed to express a *delictum dolosum,* especially in regard to the crime of homicide, and from the context of the two canons in which it is thus used alone.[82] Admittedly, *sponte* used alone does not demand the perfect *dolus* required by *sponte et scienter.* But, since even the terms now accepted as technical expressions which postulate perfect *dolus* had no fixed meaning until the Constitution *Apostolicae Sedis* (1869),[83] it seems questionable to argue, from the use of *sponte* in the *Decretum* and the decretals,[84] that its technical meaning is such as to postulate only *dolus.* Wernz-Vidal [85] and Roberti [86] both speak of this term as connoting full liberty of action. And although it is not considered expressly by pre-Code authors after the Constitution *Apos-*

mann in his review of Kuttner's *Schuldlehre-Zeitschrift d. Savigny-Stiftung, kanonistische Abtlg.,* XXV (1936), 515. Swoboda discusses the history of this canon and the dispute among the canonists as to whether the expression *"si quis suadente diabolo"* expressly postulated perfect *dolus.* His conclusion is that the more acceptable opinion seems to be that this expression did not imply the requisite of perfect *dolus.* Sipos *(Enchiridion,* p. 109) still maintains that this delict postulates perfect *dolus,* but he evidently makes no distinction between *dolus* and perfect *dolus.* It must be noted, however, that the delict always demanded an *animus iniurandi,* that is, an added quality of will consisting in the intention of harming.

[78] Canons 2322, § 2; 2345.

[79] Canon 2331, § 2.

[80] Canon 2406, § 2. Cf. Ayrinhac-Lydon, *Penal Legislation,* p. 318.

[81] *Ignorance,* p. 101.

[82] *Ignorance,* p. 102.

[83] *Fontes,* n. 552. Cf. *supra,* pp. 63-64.

[84] C. 44, D. L; c. 13, C. XXIII, q. 5; c. 110, C. XI, q. 3.

[85] *Ius Canonicum,* VII, 214.

[86] *De Delictis et Poenis,* I, 277.

tolicae Sedis, it seems that anything which would directly lessen the freedom of the will would excuse from the penalty of a law which employs the word *sponte* in qualifying the delictual act. Consequently, as regards the requirements on the part of the intellect, only a simple *dolus* is postulated by the word *sponte,* but in relation to the will an absolute freedom must be presupposed for the incurring of, or the liability for, the penalty. Thus, any factor, even such as slight fear, if it diminished this freedom, would excuse. In such a case, the action, though voluntary, lacks "spontaneity".[87]

2. *Culpa*

As already noted, the Code does not always use the term *culpa* in its specific and particular meaning as defined in canon 2199.[88] At times *culpa* and its derived forms are used for the purpose of connoting imputability.[89] In the present work the term *"culpa"* will be used in the specific meaning attached to it in canon 2199. In a *delictum culposum* the criminal deed is not directly willed, but it is the morally imputable result of a voluntary action, i.e., a voluntary neglect either to obtain the necessary knowledge or to employ the proper means to avert the harmful action.[90] In the sources of Canon Law this *culpa iuridica* is often called *negligentia* or *neglectus,*[91] *incuria,*[92] or *imperitia,* and the person to whom any *culpa* attached was said to be *incautus.*[93] That such a *delictum culposum* is a delict in the strict sense of the word is evident both from the definition of a delict [94] and from the definition of imputability.[95]

[87] Cf. Latini, *Lineamenta,* p. 118, Michiels, *De Delictis et Poenis,* I, 194-195.

[88] "Imputabilitas delicti pendet . . . vel ex eiusdem culpa in ignorantia legis violatae aut in omissione debitae diligentiae."

[89] Cf., e.g., canons 2202, § 1; 2208, § 2; 2209, §§ 1, 2, 5; 2213, § 2; 2229, § 3, 2°; 2354, § 2.

[90] Cf. Swoboda, *Ignorance,* p. 102.

[91] C. 49, D. L; c. 50, D. L; c. 7, X, *de crimine falsi,* V. 20.

[92] C. 7, X, *de poenitentiis et remissionibus,* V. 38.

[93] C. 8, X, *de homicidio voluntario vel casuali,* V, 12; cf. Michiels *De Delictis et Poenis,* I, 105; Swoboda, *Ignorance,* p. 103.

[94] Canon 2195, § 1.

[95] Canon 2199.

Canonists generally distinguish three degrees of *culpa; lata, levis* and *levissima.* This distinction was introduced into Canon Law from Roman Law by the decretists. It is found in the first commentaries on the *Decretum,*[96] and was used by canonists up to the present day.[97] Applying this ancient canonical doctrine to the present law, one finds that *culpa levissima* does not imply grave moral guilt, and hence does not come under the punishment of the law. This is clear from those provisions of the Code according to which a crime must be a matter of grave moral guilt.[98] Hence, whatever excuses from grave moral guilt excuses also from penal responsibility.

Culpa levis connotes the degree of imputability which is generally understood when the Code speaks of *culpa.* Evidently, then, *levis* in this connection does not mean slight or venial moral guilt. The term is here used in a juridical sense, and presupposes grave moral guilt.[99]

Culpa lata is the "*culpa dolo proxima*" of which mention is made in canon 2203, § 1. Such can be had only when the law is known and the effects of one's actions are known or foreseen, and when no diligence, or at least not the diligence which every prudent man would use (ordinary diligence) has been employed to prevent the criminal effects of the action.[100]

One may distinguish *culpa, dolus* and *casus* briefly as follows. In *dolus* the criminal result is both foreseen and directly willed. In *culpa* the effect is never directly willed; the effect is either foreseen but nevertheless culpably permitted because of a failure in the duty to prevent a foreseen criminal result; or the effect is due to negligence in not foreseeing the violation of the law. In *casus* there is

[96] V. g., *Summa Bambergensis* (ca. 1210) ad c. 50, D.L—Kuttner, *Schuldlehre,* pp. 219-220, note 5.

[97] Cf. Swoboda, *Ignorance,* p. 109.

[98] Canon 2218, § 2.

[99] Cf. Swoboda, *Ignorance,* p. 110. He points out that there is some flexibility in the use of these terms. What is described above as *culpa levis* may be considered *culpa lata.* In such a case the *culpa dolo proxima* mentioned in canon 2203, § 1, would then be considered distinct from *culpa lata,—Ibid.,* note 126.

[100] Canon 2203, § 1.

no moral guilt either in not preventing the injurious or anti-juridical effect or in not foreseeing the effect.[101]

The foregoing shows that *culpa* always furnishes a sufficient basis for delictual imputability.[102] That it is not sufficient for penal responsibility in those cases which postulate *dolus* or perfect *dolus* has already been pointed out. In such cases *culpa* renders the violation of the law juridically imputable, but not in a sufficient degree to entail the application of the penalty determined by the particular law.[103] As a reason for the distinction in the Code between imputability and responsibility there can be mentioned the possibility of the *actio civilis* adverted to in canon 2210, § 1, 2°, which is granted if the delict inflicts harm on a person. This possibility remains even though there is no penal responsibility for the particular delict because of the absence of *dolus* or perfect *dolus*.

Finally, it is to be noted that a *delictum culposum* is to be punished according to the degree of moral or subjective guilt. Certainly in the case of *culpa* the imputability and consequent penal responsibility is less than if the delict were committed with *dolus*.[104] In the individual case the judge must determine the measure of guilt and the consequent penalty. The law makes special provision in the case of *latae sententiae* penalties, wherein there is no judge to decide. The purpose is to protect the individual against a penalty which would be out of proportion with his subjective guilt.[105]

[101] Swoboda, *Ignorance*, p. 105.

[102] *Culpa* is also considered a basis for imputability in Criminal Law as accepted by the American Courts. The *Corpus Iuris* ([ed. Mack and Hale, New York: American Law Book Co., 1918], Vol. XVI, n. 59, p. 91) states: "Such compulsion (in order to excuse) must have arisen without the negligence or fault of the person who insists upon it as a defense."

[103] Cf. Michiels, *De Delictis et Poenis*, I, 112-113; Coronata, *Institutiones Iuris Canonici*, IV, 26-28; Swoboda, *Ignorance*, pp. 111-112. Some authors, e.g., Moersdorf (*Rechtssprache des Codex Juris Canonici*, p. 376), deny the universal imputability of delicts committed *ex culpa* inasmuch as the law sometimes presupposes *dolus* for the incurring of a penalty. The two opinions arrive at approximately the same result.

[104] Cf. canon 2203, § 1. In the case of *culpa dolo proxima* there cannot be much difference.

[105] Cf. canons 2203; 2229; Swoboda, *Ignorance*, pp. 112-113.

3. Force and Fear in Relation to *Dolus,* Perfect *Dolus* and *Culpa*

The distinction between *dolus* and *culpa* is essentially based on the intellectual quality of the will. It is the distinction between the *voluntarium directum* and the *voluntarium indirectum.* But force and fear affect the juridical imputability of an action beyond this distinction.

In the absolute, invincible force spoken of in canon 2205, § 1, there is neither *dolus* nor *culpa.* Such force which deprives a person of all freedom of action absolutely excuses, since the violence cannot be resisted and it is presumed that the agent came under such force not through his own imprudence or negligence. If the force could be resisted, there would be *dolus* in the forced action. And in the case of imprudence or negligence there would be *culpa.*[106]

Fear, even absolutely grave fear, as long as it does not impair the use of reason, does not exclude *dolus.* Nor does necessity or hardship. For if in these cases the delinquent acts as motivated by one of these factors, there is a *voluntarium directum.*[107]

It can easily be seen, then, why the distinction between *dolus* and perfect *dolus* developed particularly in the doctrine of the canonists concerning questions of ignorance relative to the incurring of ecclesiastical penalties.[108] It was to be expected that the authors would stress only ignorance as a special factor in excusing even when the terms "*praesumpserit, consulto* etc." were used in a

[106] Cf. Latini, *Lineamenta,* p. 131.

[107] The distinction between the *voluntarium directum* and the *voluntarium indirectum,* on the one hand, and the distinction between the *voluntarium simpliciter-voluntarium secundum quid* and the *involuntarium simpliciter-involuntarium secundum quid,* on the other hand, must be kept separate. The former distinction concerns the fact whether the object is willed in itself *(in se)* or in something else *(in alio),* while the latter distinction looks to the amount of voluntariness in the act. An act performed because of fear denotes a *voluntarium simpliciter* and an *involuntarium secundum quid.*

[108] Cf. Kuttner, *Schuldlehre,* pp. 74-76; Swoboda, *Ignorance,* pp. 72-74.

law or statute.[109] Even after the Constitution *Apostolicae Sedis* (1869) [110] most of the canonists neglected to consider fear as effecting a special excuse from the incurring of a penalty when the enacted penal law incorporated terms which postulated perfect *dolus* in the delictual act. In the Code there is enacted the first explicit ecclesiastical legislation in virtue of which a full freedom of will is a prerequisite condition for the incurring of any penalty whenever the violation of the penal law can be perpetrated only if it be executed with perfect *dolus*.[111]

[109] Cf. *supra*, p. 51.

[110] *Fontes*, n. 552.

[111] Canon 2229, § 2. Cf. Claeys Bouuaert, "De metus influxu quoad valorem actuum et quoad delicta et poenas secundum Codicem Iuris Canonici," *Jus Pontificum*, VI (1926), 141.

CHAPTER IV

THE NATURE AND DIVISIONS OF FORCE AND FEAR

Free will which is the principle of true human acts, is an absolute prerequisite for the commission of morally imputable delicts. Experience teaches that this necessary principle is frequently impaired in its natural operations by reason of external and internal conditions.

It can happen that the command or control which the will ordinarily exercises over the external senses and the motor centers *(vis motrix)*, and through these over the external actions, is actually frustrated because of physical violence. Such violence is a physical motion contrary to the natural inclination of the will and is exerted upon the body of the agent from without. The one upon whom this violence is exerted is physically forced to place a determined external act, or is physically impeded from externally manifesting the command of the will, or, as it is called, the internal intention.

The human will can never be forced by any external physical power to place certain internal acts. But the will, being a *potentia appetitiva,* has good as its object. This object can be proposed either by reason or by the sensitive appetency. And the will naturally moves in that direction in which either reason or sensitive appetency inclines it by offering the appearance of good. Hence it frequently happens that the will, because of a concurrence of peculiar circumstances, determines itself either through the judgment of reason or the impulse of the sensitive appetency to something to which it would never have determined itself under normal circumstances. In such a case this movement *(determinatio)* is said to take place under moral force or violence *(violentia moralis)*. This act of the will considered in itself is evidently voluntary, but as the Scholastics termed it, involuntary *secundum quid.* As Latini (1857-1938) expressed it, such a determination of the will elicited under moral force is indeed voluntary, but not spontaneous.[1]

[1] *Lineamenta,* p. 118. Cf. Michiels, *De Delictis et Poenis,* I, 194-195.

Such moral violence by which the will is forced to place some act which is materially or of its own objectiveness criminal, can be effected by the misguided dictate either of reason or of the sensitive appetency. It is occasioned by the sensitive appetency when the object of the volition which is in itself and ontologically a bad object is represented to the will as a good object inasmuch as the indwelling propensities of the senses prevail over the enlightened dictates of reason.[2] This is the case when the will is moved to a criminal act under the influence of passion. The moral violence to the will is occasioned by reason when the object of the volition which is otherwise evil, and hence despicable, appears as an object that is good and hence desirable, because of the concurrence of certain circumstances. This is the case when a man sees himself in a state of so-called "conditional necessity". In such circumstances he finds it impossible to avoid a threatened evil, or to defend his rights, or to fulfill his legal duties, unless he places an act which is materially criminal *(in se spectatus)*.

When this conditional necessity is caused by a free human cause extrinsic to the agent, that is, by one who unjustly threatens the evil, there is present the case of fear smitten unjustly upon the agent *(metus iniuste incussus)*. Sometimes this conditional necessity arises from some objective condition of things, or from a conflict that exists between the juridic duty incumbent upon a person and his legal claims vesting in goods, be they spiritual or corporal. In such an instance there is a case of necessity properly so-called, or as the Code expresses it, *necessitas* or *grave incommodum*. The case of legitimate defense is verified when this necessity arises from an unjust aggression so that the agent feels necessitated to place an act which is in itself delictual, that is, materially criminal, in order to defend himself.[3]

Article I. Force

I. The Nature of Force

Force, the English equivalent of *vis* or *violentia*, signifies either

[2] Cf. Latini, *Lineamenta*, p. 119.

[3] Cf. Michiels, *De Delictis et Poenis*, I, 194-196; Wernz-Vidal, *Ius Canonicum*, VI, 101-103.

strength and might *(vis)*, or the exerting of them upon another *(violentia)*. In the Roman Law sources *vis* signified the impetus exerted by the external thing.[4] This meaning of *vis* was accepted by the early decretists.[5] Violence may be defined as the using of such an 'impetus' to compel another to perform an action against his will.[6] These two significations of force are simple and do not cause any serious problem either in themselves or in their application to the question of imputability.

II. The Divisions of Force

The older canonists first used the term *coactio* to designate both force and fear. This was distinguished first according to degrees, *modica* and *violenta,* then according to species,*absoluta* and *conditionalis.*[7] Later St. Raymond of Penyafort (+1275) differentiated the *vis levis* and the *vis violenta.*[8] This division, which was adopted by the later canonists and moralists, is substantially the same as that which is in use today.

Absolute physical violence *(vis violenta)* is that which takes away all liberty of action—*"omnem adimit agendi facultatem"*,[9] and is described in canon 103, § 1, as an "extrinsic force which cannot be resisted." [10] When the term violence is used by modern moralists or canonists, it is usually this absolute physical force that is meant.

The slight force *(vis levis)* mentioned by St. Raymond denotes all such external force which does not take away all freedom of action and therefore can be externally resisted. It is a force the effects of which can be withstood. It is referred to as a relative force *(violentia secundum quid)*. Since this relative force is not expressly mentioned in the Code, it will be better to consider it under the heading of "necessity." One smitten with such force

[4] D. (4.2) 2 (Paulus: definition of *vis maior)*.
[5] Cf. *supra,* p. 10.
[6] Cf. Ayrinhac-Lydon, *Penal Legislation,* p. 12.
[7] Cf. *supra,* pp. 5-6.
[8] Cf. *supra,* p. 27.
[9] Canon 2205, § 1.
[10] *"cui resisti non potest"*.

is surely in the position of one who is in physical necessity, either slight or grave. Hence the norms referrible to a person who is in necessity can also be applied to one who is under duress of vincible physical force.

For the sake of clarity and in order to conform to the usage of modern canonists and moralists, the word "force" or "violence", unless the contrary be noted, will be used here simply in the sense of absolute physical force.

Article II. Fear

I. *The Nature of Fear*

In general, fear, an irascible passion, arises in the sensitive appetency from the representation of some evil. Just as the evil which is feared may be either of a sensible or of a spiritual character, so also the faculty which fears the evil and tries to flee from it can be either the sensitive appentency or the rational (spiritual) inclination, the will. Often both faculties are affected. Now, if this fear is prevalent in the sensitive appetency, it produces the same effects as any other motion of the sensitive appetency, i.e., it lessens deliberation and freedom, or takes them away altogether if it is vehement, and especially if it emerges suddenly. If this fear prevails merely in the rational faculty, then the person remains free and freely seeks the means to escape the imminent evil by choosing a lesser evil.[11] This latter fear is the *metus* considered by canonists. The former type of fear excuses from all imputability if it takes away deliberation and freedom completely.[12]. But if enough deliberation remains to make an act gravely sinful, then the fear is considered as an excusing factor only in proportion to its gravity as perceived by the intellect. In the present work consideration will be given solely to that fear which affects the rational faculty.

[11] Cf. Noldin-Schmitt, *Summa Theologiae Moralis* (3 vols, Vol. I, 23. ed., Oeniponte: Rauch, 1935), I, p. 62, n. 54.

[12] Cf. Ayrinhac—Lydon, *Penal Legislation*, p. 15; Sole, *De Delictis et Poenis* (Romae: Pustet, 1920), p. 26.

Fear *(metus)*, which was often referred to by the older decretists [13] as a conditional, moral or compelling *(compulsiva)* force "*quae facit necessitatem conditionatam,*" consists in moral coercion, in the threat of some imminent evil. The mind, being disturbed by the dread of some imminent evil which it desires to avoid, is moved or compelled to will something which it would not otherwise will. Thus fear in the active sense is really the objective cause of the passive fear produced *(metus passive sumptus)*. This passive fear in turn conditionally forces the subject to place a certain act in order to avoid an imminent danger.

Canonists since Alexander III (1159-1181) [14] generally define fear (in the passive sense) as "a confusion or perturbation of the mind caused by instant or future danger".[15] It is called a confusion or perturbation of the mind *(mentis trepidatio)* to indicate that it is an affection of the mind or will *(affectio animi)*. As Roberti points out, it is an irascible passion in regard to the evil from which one flees.[16] Now, of itself (abstracting from the physical and organic movements mentioned above), fear does not impede the objective and deliberate judgment of our reason. Nor does it take away our fullness of choice, but leaves freedom intact. For, one who acts through fear actually selects with a free choice what seems to him a lesser evil, even though he would not select to submit to it if fear were not present. But this fear does modify the *voluntarium* in so far as it modifies the object of the act of the will, and thus makes it, as S. Thomas termed it, an *involuntarium secundum quid*. According to the canonists, such an act does not lack liberty, but spontaneity.[17]

The words "*instantis vel futuri periculi*" are stressed by some to show that this perturbation has to be really the effect of an imminent evil.[18] This seems to show that the influence of the canonical doctrine on contracts eventually also affected the canoni-

[13] Cf. *supra*, p. 8.

[14] Cf. *supra*, p. 10.

[15] This is the definition given by Ulpian—D. (4.2) 1.

[16] *De Delictis et Poenis*, I, 151.

[17] Cf. Wernz-Vidal, *Ius Canonicum*, VII, 103; Claeys Bouuaert, *art. cit.—Jus Pontificium*, VI (1926), 106; Latini, *Lineamenta*, p. 118.

[18] E. g., Michiels, *De Delictis et Poenis*, I, 198.

cal doctrine in matters of the penal laws.[19] But, as regards juridical imputability and consequent penal responsibility, the excusing effect of fear seems to be just as valid if the evil does not actually impend, provided that there is a real perturbation because of an imagined evil. This fear would then be equivalent to an imagined necessity.[20] The problem of proving such an imagined necessity in the external forum is a difficult one, but a valid excuse would certainly be had in the internal forum.

II. The Divisions of Fear

Canonists distinguish fear in respect to its cause, in relation to the manner in which it is inflicted, and with reference to the amount of perturbation it effects, or, in other words, with a view to its gravity.[21]

1. Division of Fear in Respect to Its Cause

A division of fear stressed by Sporer (+1683) [22] was that which divided fear into *metus ab intrinseco* and *metus ab extrinseco.* Fear from within *(ab intrinseco)* is usually defined as that fear which arises either from some cause internal to the person or from some external necessary cause, or some natural event, whose existence is not dependent on a free human agent. An instance of fear arising from a cause within the agent is fear from sickness. An earthquake, a fire and a shipwreck may be cited as examples of an external necessary cause of fear.

Fear from without *(ab extrinseco)* is such as is caused by a free created cause, a free human agent. Such fear arises from the threats of another man. This fear from without is the only fear considered explicitly as fear by canonists in the problem of

[19] Cf. *supra*, p. 39.

[20] It should be noted that the question of full excuse will depend also on whether the fear was imagined through culpable or inculpable error.

[21] Cf. Wernz-Vidal, *Ius Canonicum*, VII, 104; *Schmalzgrueber*, lib. I, tit. XL, n. 2; Michiels, *De Delictis et Poenis*, I, 198; *supra*, p. 37.

[22] *Theologia Moralis*, I, n. 156—*supra*, pp. 36-37.

imputability and responsibility. Fear from within is considered rather as an instance of necessity and is correspondingly treated under the heading of necessity.[23]

2. *Division of Fear in Relation to the Manner in Which It Is Inflicted*

The terms "just fear" and "unjust fear" have not always had the same meaning in canonical writings. The first time the expressions *metus iustus* and *metus iniustus* occur in the writings of the decretists they are synonymous with *metus qui caderet in virum constantem* and *metus qui non caderet in virum constantem.*[24] Later the terms "just" and "unjust" came to be used exclusively in relation to the manner in which the fear was inflicted.[25]

Fear is said to be unjustly inflicted when the threatened evil is in some way unjust. This evil can be unjust considered in itself *(quoad substantiam)*. Such is the case when the threatened evil is an injury to the right of the agent or of some one closely connected with him, when such an injury is in no wise deserved, or when it is inflicted without a just cause.[26]

Fear may be unjust also in view of the concrete circumstances in which it is inflicted. Such can be the case even though the evil which is threatened or inflicted is in itself just. Thus, if the one inflicting the fear has no competence in the matter, or, even though he be competent, threatens the evil in an illegitimate manner. For example, a father threatens one who has promised marriage to his daughter but will not fulfill the promise that he will take revenge privately and independently of competent authority.[27] Another instance of fear that is unjust *quoad modum* is had when

[23] Cf. Wernz-Vidal, *Ius Canonicum,* VII, 106-109; Vermeersch ("De Metu qui, saltem ex lege positiva, excusat ab obligationibus vitiato consensu susceptis, praecipue de metu ab intrinseco vel extrinseco.") *Periodica,* XVII (1928), 138*-144*.

[24] Cf. *supra,* p. 12.

[25] Cf. *supra,* p. 37.

[26] Cf. Michiels, *De Delictis et Poenis,* I, 198.

[27] Cf. Sipos, *Enchiridion,* p. 94.

the intention of the one inflicting the fear is unjust, as, for example, when the fear is inflicted to extort a criminal act.[28]

The essential characteristic of unjust fear seems to lie in the disproportion between end and means. This is seen clearly in typical cases of blackmail. The Code itself does not make the distinction between just and unjust fear in regard to imputability. But it seems evident that a fear which directly impels one to the violation of a penal law can never be just on the part of the one inflicting it.[29]

Fear is said to be directly inflicted when it is intended for the sake of extorting some particular action. It is indirectly inflicted when the intention of the one who inflicts it tends not to any determined particular action to be placed by the one suffering the fear.[30] If the fear is inflicted indirectly (whether justly or unjustly) and the agent chooses to violate the law rather than to submit to the thing threatened or its alternative, then the case is rather one of necessity and the excusing effect would have to be judged according to the norms governing the factor of necessity. An example of this case would be verified in the unjust withholding from pious institutes of goods whose payment could be rendered,[31] in order to pay, with what is thus withheld, some extraneous bill when one is threatened with a court case if that bill is not paid.

3. Division of Fear With Reference to Its Quantity or Degree

The only degree of fear admitted by the early canonists as diminishing responsibility was that "which would influence a resolute man" *(qui caderet in virum constantem)*.[32] But it must be borne in mind that these canonists were not concerned with criminal legal problems when they employed this distinction. They treated rather the question of the validity of legal actions (resig-

[28] Michiels, *De Delictis et Poenis*, I, 198.

[29] Cf. Wernz-Vidal, Ius Canonicum, VII, 106; Oesterle, "Ex Privata Jurisprudentia,"—*Jus Pontificium*, X (1930), 250.

[30] Cf. Roberti, "De Metu Indirecto quoad Negotia Iuridica praesertim Matrimonium,"—*Apollinaris*, XI (1938), 559.

[31] Canon 2348.

[32] Cf. *supra*, pp. 12-13.

nations, vows, etc.) as well as the question of justified protection against extorted legal claims.[33] Later, as the moralists and canonists turned more to the question of excuse or pardon for a forced delinquent, there can be noted the appearance of the term "relatively grave fear", (sometimes referred to as *metus vanus)* in its capacity of a partially excusing factor.[34] By the time of St. Alphonsus (1696-1787) the terms "absolutely grave fear," "relatively grave fear," and "slight fear" were clearly defined and agreed upon by the moralists.[35]

Grave fear is defined as such that would certainly influence and deter a prudent and resolute man from his resolve.[36] But since fear is essentially a subjective affection of the mind caused by some threat of evil, it is evident that the gravity of the fear must be judged not exclusively, nor even primarily, from the objective gravity of the evil threatened, but principally from the individual temperament, the subjective nature of the person who actually suffers the evil of fear.

Thus the authors commonly teach that the same standard or measure cannot always be used in judging the degree of the fear, but that various circumstances must be considered in each instance. The first requirement for the gravity of fear is that the evil which is feared be grave in itself or objectively, at least in respect to the one suffering the fear. Some evils are considered to be "absolutely grave" or by their very nature to be such as would influence any man whatsoever. Such evils are presumed to produce grave fear always and for everyone. Examples of such

[33] Cf. *supra,* p. 14.

[34] Cf. Ioannes Andreae, (+1348), *Novella* ad c. 5, X, *de his quae vi metusve causa fiunt,* I, 40; *supra,* p. 30.

[35] Cf. Schmalzgrueber, (+1735), lib. I, tit. XL, n. 2; St. Alphonsus, *Theologia Moralis,* lib. III, tract. V, cap. III, n. 718; *supra,* pp. 40-41.

[36] These same notions have been carried over into secular law. "An act which would otherwise constitute a crime may also be excused on the ground that it was done under compulsion or duress. The compulsion which will excuse a criminal act, however, must be present, imminent, and impending, and of such a nature as to induce a well-grounded apprehension of death or serious bodily harm if the act is not done. A threat of future injury is not enough."—*Corpus Iuris,* Vol. XVI, n. 59, p. 91.

evils are death, exile, rapé, loss of liberty. This presumption stands also if the evil is threatened to persons who are closely connected with the victim of the fear, e.g., to his parents, to his wife, etc. Other evils, which are considered slight if taken absolutely or by themselves, can be relatively grave in respect to a determined person. For the gravity of the subjective affections, in which fear essentially consists, depends mostly on the physical and psychological make-up of the individual victim, which characteristic can vary greatly according to sex, age, general health, strength of mind, integrity of character, range of education, etc.

Finally, for grave fear it is always required that the victim of it cannot easily avoid the threatened evil in any other way than by means of the materially criminal action.[87]

Slight fear, then, arises either from a slightness in the evil which is threatened, or from a gravity in the evil which may however be easily avoided, or which is at most only dubiously threatened.[88]

Article III. Necessity and Hardship

1. The Nature of Necessity and Hardship

A concept allied to those of force and fear is that of necessity. In penal law necessity may be defined as that objective condition of things, brought about in any manner whatsoever, in which an act that according to penal law is to be placed or omitted cannot be so placed or omitted because of an absolute or moral powerlessness, whether this latter be physical or spiritual.[89] In necessity the danger arises from the objective condition of things, for example, from the forces of nature, the lack of the means necessary for life, etc.

Necessity is distinguished from force, for force takes away all freedom of the will, the will being completely subjected, whereas in necessity the will remains free, but the act is placed for the sake

[87] Cf. Michiels, *De Delictis et Poenis,* I, 199.

[88] Cf. Noldin-Schmitt, *Summa Theologiae Moralis,* I, 63.

[89] Cf. Michiels, *De Delictis et Poenis,* I, 199; Wernz-Vidal *(Ius Canonicum,* VIII, 107) define it as the presence of danger or the imminence of evil neither just nor legitimate.

of protecting one's rights. It is distinguished from fear *(metus ab extrinseco),* for the latter is induced by a free human agent who threatens a certain evil. And it is distinct from unjust aggression, for here again there is question of a free human agent, a person who inflicts the actual harm.

Grave hardship *(grave incommodum)* is relative necessity or moral impossibility. Canonists consider the role of fear from within *(ab intrinseco),* that is, both the fear arising from an interior cause and also the fear arising from a necessary exterior cause, under the heading of necessity and grave hardship.[40]

II. The Divisions of Necessity

1. Division of Necessity According To Its Nature

Spiritual necessity is that which thrusts the agent into the position of necessarily having to choose between some harm to his own soul or the souls of others and the violation of some penal law.

Physical necessity is that which either impedes one from observing the law because of a lack of strength or of natural means, or places one in a position in which it is necessary to choose between the violation of the law and some grave physical hardship or notable damage to natural goods or interests.

2. Division of Necessity According To Its Degree

Some authors divide necessity into absolute necessity and moral necessity. Thus absolute spiritual necessity is present when a law cannot be observed without the commission of a material sin. This is verified in a case wherein there is a conflict between a duty imposed by penal law and a command enjoined by legitimate authority. Absolute physical necessity is present when one lacks absolutely the strength or the natural means for fulfilling the law.

Moral spiritual necessity is present when a determined penal law cannot be observed without serious harm to the soul of the agent or of another, for example, because of scruples arising therefrom or because of imminent scandal. Moral physical necessity is present when there is made necessary a choice between the viola-

[40] Cf., e.g., Wernz-Vidal, *Ius Canonicum,* VII, 106-107.

tion of the law and the suffering of some grave physical hardship or serious damage to natural goods, such as health or fortune.[41]

A similar division of necessity is that of extreme, grave and slight necessity. Slight or ordinary necessity is that which does not occasion grave hardship, or, if grave hardship be present, the conditions are such that one can be freed of it without serious difficulty. Grave necessity is that in which an absolutely or relatively grave evil impends and cannot be avoided, or, if it can be avoided, then only with great difficulty and through the use of some extraordinary means. Extreme necessity is that which places one in danger of life, or of some equivalent good, in such a way that this cannot be avoided without transgressing the penal law or perhaps by some other very extraordinary means.[42]

Grave hardship *(grave incommodum)*, as noted above, is termed relative necessity or moral impossibility, and is governed by the same norms which obtain in relation to necessity. These same norms will also obtain in relation to fear from within *(ab intrinseco)*, for this kind of fear is comprised in the general notion of necessity or grave hardship.

[41] Michiels, *De Delictis et Poenis*, I, 199-200.
[42] Wernz-Vidal, *Ius Canonicum*, VII, 107.

CHAPTER V

THE EFFECTS OF FORCE AND FEAR UPON DELICTUAL IMPUTABILITY

As noted in the historical commentary of the present work, the canonical doctrine on criminal imputability and penal responsibility in the case of force and fear has developed very gradually from the discussions and comments of the canonists on the rôle of these two factors in the field of contracts. Now, in the present Code of Canon Law, there exists the first general legislation for delictual imputability and penal responsibility in cases of force and fear. But, as will be noted later, the present terminology and divisions used in the Code show definite traces of this relation to the law of contracts. Thus the legal principles and terminology, although now clearly defined, will have to be explained in view of this historical development. There remain for discussion also several specific problems of interpretation.

The present chapter treats of these factors in relation to criminal imputability in general. The application of the rules, as here explained, to responsibility in cases of *ferendae sententiae* penalties and *latae sententiae* penalties will be discussed in the following chapters.

Article I. The Imputability of Delicts Committed Because of Force

According to canon 2205, § 1, physical violence which deprives a person of all freedom of action absolutely excuses from imputability, or in other words entirely precludes a delict.[1] This principle regarding complete excuse in the case of absolute physical force is clearly founded upon the natural law and expression is given to it both in canonical legislation[2] and doctrine.[3] This principle

[1] "Vis physica quae omnem adimit agendi facultatem, delictum prorsus excludit."

[2] Cf., e.g., c. 32, § 2, D. L.; c. 38, X, *de sententia excommunicationis*, V. 39; c. 5, X, *de his quae vi metusve causa fiunt*, I, 40.

[3] Cf. the classical commentators on c. 5, X, *de his quae vi metusve causa fiunt*, I, 40; also Latini, *Lineamenta*, p. 131; Michiels, *De Delictis et Poenis*, I, 196-197.

really needs no explanation or proof, for an act which is performed in consequence of absolute force, when one's will is positively set against the performance of such an act, strictly considered is the act of the one who perpetrates the force, and not of the one who is constrained to submit to it. Thus the decretals spoke of such a one as being acted upon, rather than as acting.[4]

The wording of canon 2205, § 1, clearly postulates absolute physical force for the complete preclusion of a delict, such force, namely, as deprives a person of all freedom of action,[5] or, as is stated in canon 103, § 1, "an external force which cannot be resisted".[6] Such absolute force which precludes a delict completely is had only when the person is truly unable to resist and moreover did not fall into such circumstances through his own imprudence or negligence.[7] If the force can be resisted, or if there is some freedom of action, or if the effects of the force could be impeded, then the force is called moderate or slight.[8] Here the imputability is not always taken away completely, but may exist in greater or lesser degree according to the amount of guilty negligence in not resisting, etc.[9] Moreover, this slight or moderate force does not of itself preclude *dolus.*

As an excuse from imputability, the slight or moderate force *(vis modica)* can be classed as a necessity or a hardship, grave or slight according to the nature of the force. Thus it will excuse from both imputability and responsibility according to the norms given below in relation to necessity and hardship.

Finally, in the case of one falling into invincible force through one's own negligence or imprudence, there is a question of *culpa* and not of *dolus.* In such an instance, although the imputability is not completely taken away, it exists in greater or lesser degree according to the amount of the *culpa.*

[4] " . . . magis pati quam agere convincatur."—c. 5, X, *de his quae vi metusve causa fiunt,* I, 40.

[5] " . . . quae omnem adimit agendi facultatem.

[6] " . . . cui resisti non possit."

[7] Cf. Latini, *Lineamenta,* p. 131.

[8] Cf. *supra,* pp. 5-6.

[9] Cf. Sole, *De Delictis et Poenis,* p. 26; Michiels, *De Delictis et Poenis,* I, 197.

ARTICLE II. THE IMPUTABILITY OF DELICTS COMMITTED BECAUSE OF FEAR

Imputability in case of fear is treated in canon 2205, §§ 2, 3. There it is stated that grave fear, even when only relatively grave, excuses as a rule from all imputability when there is question of purely ecclesiastical laws. However, if an act is intrinsically evil, or involves contempt of the faith or of ecclesiastical authority, or works to the detriment of souls, then excuses based on grave fear diminish but do not destroy imputability.[10]

The legislator here follows the pre-Code doctrine which distinguished between merely ecclesiastical penal laws, whose observance in a concrete case was made binding solely by ecclesiastical authority, and penal laws which were not merely ecclesiastical, and whose observance was made binding by divine authority. In the latter supposition the binding obligation could arise by reason of the object of the law, i.e., when the prohibited acts were intrinsically evil. It could also arise by reason of the concrete circumstances in which the act was actually perpetrated when it was prohibited purely by ecclesiastical authority, as when the transgression redounded to a contempt of the faith or of ecclesiastical authority, or also when it turned to the detriment of souls.

I. Delictual Acts Prohibited by Purely Ecclesiastical Laws

In penal laws which derive solely from ecclesiastical authority grave fear, even if only relatively grave, usually takes away the delict completely. The reason for this is that purely ecclesiastical laws, as all other merely human laws, in case of serious inconvenience or in danger of grave harm not only do not urge *sub gravi,* which according to canon 2218, § 2, is postulated for penal responsibility, but simply do not oblige at all. For in order that a law oblige it must be reasonable; and just as a superior cannot

[10] § 2. "Metus quoque gravis, etiam relative tantum, . . . plerumque delictum, si agatur de legibus mere ecclesiasticis, penitus toll(it).

§ 3. "Si vero actus sit intrinsece malus aut vergat in contemptum fidei vel ecclesiasticae auctoritatis vel in animarum damnum, causae, de quibus in § 2, delicti imputabilitatem minuunt quidem, sed non auferunt."

impose an obligation upon a whole community when its observance is beyond the ordinary powers of the members of the community, so neither can he demand the observance of a law in those circumstances in which the observance would work too great a hardship. In fact, the very foundation of juridic-criminal imputability is lacking in these cases, so that not only is culpability taken away, but even the delict itself is removed.[11] When the presence of grave fear creates a serious hardship for the observance of the law then the case becomes one which is not covered by the law, since the subjective legal obligation extends only to such things as are morally possible of accomplishment.[12]

The same principle applies in the case of grave fear in relation to an affirmative divine positive or natural law, for God is not presumed to oblige one under such a great hardship. Thus one is not held to the material integrity of confession, or to the restoration of ill-gotten goods in the face of grave fear.

The fear mentioned here must be at least relatively grave, that is, in respect to the person suffering the fear, and must be unjustly exerted. It should be added that this fear must be proportionately grave also in relation to the evil effects of the violation of the law.[13]

The Code states that such fear "as a rule" *(plerumque)* takes away the delict completely. This is noted because the legislator can at times and for exceptional reasons bind his subjects "*sub gravi*" to perform more difficult and arduous duties, and hence can urge the observance of some law notwithstanding the grave fear or any similar factor which is present. In fact, the Church does at times prescribe such actions, either because of some extraordinary demand of the public good or because of the character of a state of office freely assumed, as, for example, the priestly office, or the religious state, or the office of pastor. Thus a pastor

[11] Cf. Salmanticenses, *Cursus Theologicus*, vol. V, tract. X, art. VI, n. 15; Pirhing, lib. I, tit. XL, n. 3.

[12] Cf. Michiels, *De Delictis et Poenis*, I, 206; Ayrinhac-Lydon *(Penal Legislation*, p. 12) give the example of the law which commands fasting before the reception of Holy Communion.

[13] Wernz-Vidal, *Ius Canonicum*, VII, 101.

at times of pestilence must dispense the sacraments to those who are infected with the virulent disease even though there be grave personal danger involved for him. Likewise must he do so in the face of grave threats. In such cases neither grave fear, nor grave hardship, nor even necessity takes away the delict for these factors do not take away the grave obligation of the law whose violation constitutes the juridic foundation of criminal imputability or responsibility for a penalty.

Slight fear unjustly inflicted by a free human agent does not excuse from serious obligations, such as are considered in the penal law. However, such fear does diminish imputability, for it lessens the *voluntarium* and hence the gravity of the sin in proportion to its influence upon the will. To what extent this slight fear can and must be admitted as an excusing factor in the external forum will be discussed later in the chapters on responsibility for penalties.

II. Delictual Acts Interdicted by Divine Authority

When an act is intrinsically evil, or involves contempt of the faith or of ecclesiastical authority, or works to the detriment of souls, grave fear, does not take away the imputability of the delict.[14] Imputability is not taken away in such cases since in these instances the observance of the law still urges under pain of sin, even though the most severe personal hardship or danger, or also the greatest private harm might come from such observance. And the reason for this is that some spiritual good, either of God, or of the Church, or of individual souls is involved. Such a good is essentially superior to the private, natural good of the agent and therefore must be obtained at all costs. There is consequently always grave guilt in the deliberate transgression of such a law. And when this grave fault is present there is the juridic foundation for criminal imputability. This was well expressed by Pope Innocent III (1198-1216) when he insisted that "although fear lessens the fault, it does not completely exclude it, since for no fear whatsoever should one incur mortal sin." [15]

[14] Canon 2205, § 3.

[15] C. 5, X, *de his quae vi metusve causa fiunt,* I, 40; Sole, *De Delictis*

Fear, however, does diminish criminal imputability in the above mentioned cases.[16] As previously mentioned, such a factor makes the act involuntary *secundum quid,* or in other words it affects the act in such a way that it is not spontaneous. Thus the violation of a law which in its authoritative character is not merely ecclesiastical, when done under grave fear is to be punished less severely. In fact, the legislator can in his benignity decree that certain penalties such as, for instance, *latae sententiae* penalties, would not be incurred in such a case of diminished imputability. For justice does not demand that every gravely sinful act be punished. Canon 2229 shows just when a *latae sententiae* punishment is incurred in these instances.

1. Acts Intrinsically Evil

Intrinsically evil acts are distinguished from those acts which are extrinsically or merely positively evil acts. Their immoral character is so indelibly proper to them by their very nature that they cannot be made objectively good, not even by divine power. And therefore those causes which are admitted as exempting from merely positive laws, such causes namely as abrogation, dispensation, contrary custom, *epikeia,* can never take away the objective immorality of such intrinsically evil acts. Of course, in individual cases there may be excusing factors, such as error, perturbation of the mind, etc. which can take away or diminish the subjective culpability.[17]

et Poenis, p. 29; Michiels, *De Delicitis et Poenis,* I, 209.

A surprisingly similar statement is contained in the dicta of an American Court. "It must be obvious to the deliberate judgment of every reflecting mind that much less freedom of will is requisite to render a person responsible for a crime than to bind him by a sale or other contract. To overcome the will so far as to render it incapable of contracting a civil obligation, is a mere trifle compared with reducing it to that degree of slavery and submission which will exempt from punishment."—McCoy *vs.* State, 78 Georgia, 490, 497, 3 S. E. 768; cf. *Corpus Iuris,* Vol. XVI, n. 59, p. 91.

[16] " . . . delicti imputabilitatem minuunt quidem."—canon 2205, § 3.

[17] Michiels, *De Delictis et Poenis,* I, 210; Sole, *De Delictis et Poenis,* p. 28.

In general it can be said that all acts contrary to the fundamental precepts of the natural law are intrinsically evil. Thus the following are included in this category; blasphemy, perjury,[18] idolatry, superstition, sacrilege,[19] abortion,[20] murder,[21] theft, fornication. Apostasy, heresy and schism must also be classed as intrinsically evil.[22] It must perhaps remain a matter of dispute whether the various falsifications contained under the canonical "*crimen falsi*" would come under this classification.[23]

2. *Acts Involving Contempt of the Faith or of Ecclesiastical Authority*

This and the following enumeration of acts which work to the detriment of souls may seem superfluous since they are already, by their very notion, intrinsically evil and hence included in the category above. Claeys Bouuaert points out that the reason for this enumeration is to indicate those acts which are intrinsically evil not so much because of their subject matter but because of their end or circumstances and because many of these are punished with determined penalties in the Code itself.[24]

In order to identify the various acts that are to be classified in this category, a close study of the terms used is necessary. First, it must be stressed that the contempt of the faith or of authority mentioned here must not be understood as subjective contempt formally present in the intention of the agent. It is rather the objective contempt resulting from the very nature of the act, or at least from the concrete circumstances in which the act is placed. The legislator indicates this by speaking of the act which tends to such contempt, and not of the contempt of the agent.[25]

[18] Canon 2323.

[19] Canon 2325.

[20] Canon 2350, § 1.

[21] Canon 2354.

[22] Canon 2314.

[23] Canons 2360; 2405; 2406.

[24] "De metus influxu quoad valorem actuum et quoad delicta et poenas secundum Codicem Iuris Canonici."—*Jus Pontificium,* VI (1926), 138.

[25] Michiels, *De Delictis et Poenis,* I, 210.

It must be stressed also that not every lack of reverence or of honor, nor every disobedience to ecclesiastical authority, can be called contempt in the sense understood by the Code; otherwise fear would never excuse from a delict, since every violation of an ecclesiastical penal law implicitly involves some contempt of authority. Clearly, then, the concept of this contempt must be restricted so as to include only those delicts which involve contempt of the faith or of authority in a special manner. This will be the case either because they are of their very nature directly aimed against the truths of faith or against persons constituted in authority, or because they violate a precept in such a way that by reason of circumstances such contempt necessarily and directly redounds to faith or to authority.[26]

The Code does not give an exhaustive list of such acts which of their very nature involve this special contempt of the faith or of ecclesiastical authority. Titles XI and XII of the Fifth Book of the Code contain the acts which tend toward contempt of the faith. These Titles are inscribed "Delicts against the Faith and Unity of the Church," [27] and "Delicts against Religion." [28] But not all the delicts mentioned in these Titles can be said to involve such contempt of the faith as is understood in canon 2205, § 3. In seeking to establish just what acts contain this contempt, it is necessary to bear in mind the general rule of canon 2219. There it is stated that in penalties the milder interpretation is to be applied. So in case of doubt as to whether an act objectively connotes such contempt, the act is to be considered as not involving it. There are certain crimes included in Titles XI and XII which do not seem to involve this contempt in their very notion. Such are the defense of certain condemned doctrines which however are not branded as heretical; [29] the printing of books of Sacred Scripture without permission; [30] illegal bination and the break-

[26] Cf. Roberti, *De Delictis et Poenis,* I, 152; Michiels, *De Delictis et Poenis,* I, 210-211; Claeys Bouuaert, *art. cit.—Jus Pontificium,* VI (1926), 138-139.

[27] Canons 2314-2319.

[28] Canons 2320-2329.

[29] Canon 2317.

[30] Canon 2318, § 2.

ing of the natural fast before the celebration of Mass; [31] blasphemy and perjury; [32] offenses against the laws on Mass stipends; [33] the trafficking in indulgences; [34] the violation of corpses or graves,[35] and the violation of churches or cemeteries.[36]

The following crimes seem necessarily to involve this special contempt in their very concept; the crime of apostasy, heresy or schism; [37] spontaneous assistance in the propagation of heresy, and communication in sacred rites with heretics; [38] the publishing, defending, conscious reading or retaining without due permission of the books of apostates, heretics, schismatics, in defense of apostasy etc.; [39] the celebration of mixed marriages before a non-Catholic minister, and the non-Catholic baptism or education of children;[40] the casting away of the Sacred Species, or the carrying of them off or the retaining of them for an evil purpose; [41] the usurpation of priestly functions; [42] superstition and sacrilege; [43] the making of false relics, and the conscious selling, distributing or exposing of such.[44]

[31] Canon 2321.

[32] Canon 2323. These two crimes are of course intrinsically evil, but they do not contain this special contempt. This distinction is of importance for determining in how far the incurring of the penalty will obtain if the penalty if of a *latae sententiae* character.

[33] Canon 2324.

[34] Canon 2327.

[35] Canon 2328.

[36] Canon 2329.

[37] Canon 2314, § 1.

[38] Canon 2316.

[39] Canon 2318, § 1.

[40] Canon 2319. It seems probable that disparate marriages before a non-Catholic minister are not included under the penalty of canon 2319. Cf. Eichmann, *Das Strafrecht des Codex Iuris Canonici* (Paderborn: Schöningh, 1920), pp. 132-133; also *Quinquennial Faculties of Ordinaries:* Latest Formula for the United States—Faculties from the Holy Office, nn. 2, 3—Bouscaren, *The Canon Law Digest* (2 vols., Milwaukee: The Bruce Publishing Co., 1934-1943) Vol. II, pp. 30-31.

[41] Canon 2320.

[42] Canon 2322.

[43] Canon 2325.

[44] Canon 2326.

The acts which of their nature tend toward contempt of ecclesiastical authority are contained in Title XIII of the Fifth Book of the Code.[45] Here again, however, there are mentioned certain criminal acts which do not contain the special contempt understood by canon 2205, § 3. Such contempt is present only in those delicts which involve a contemning of authority in a special manner, either because they are aimed directly against persons in authority or against their authority as such, or because they formally violate some command in such a way that the authority itself is necessarily and directly contemned.[46]

This contempt is found in the crime of conspiracy against the authority of the Roman Pontiff or his legates, or against one's own Ordinary as outlined in canon 2331, § 2. This is also the case in an appeal from the decrees of the Roman Pontiff to a universal Council; [47] in recourse to the civil power against the letters or acts of the Apostolic See or of its legates;[48] in interference with the liberty and rights of the Church as outlined in canon 2334; in the crime of pastors and of other priests who incite the people to interfere with ecclesiastical jurisdiction; [49] in ordering or forcing ecclesiastical burial against the prohibition of the Church; [50] in violating the privilege of the ecclesiastical forum; [51] in violating the *privilegium canonis* by assaulting the Roman Pontiff, his legate, or one's own ordinary; [52] in heaping verbal abuse and injury upon the last-named persons.[53] But there seems to be no such contempt of ecclesiastical authority in the violation of the *privilegium canonis* or in the perpetration of verbal abuse or injury against other ecclesiastics who have no authority over the delinquent.

Among the crimes mentioned in Title XIII the following do not seem to imply this special contempt; enrollment in the sect

[45] Canons 2330-2349.
[46] Cf. Claeys Bouuaert, *art. cit.,—Jus Pontificium,* VI (1926), 139.
[47] Canon 2332.
[48] Canon 2333.
[49] Canon 2337.
[50] Canon 2339.
[51] Canon 2341.
[52] Canon 2343.
[53] Canon 2344.

of the Freemasons and in similar societies; [54] unauthorized absolution from excommunication, participation in the crime of an *excommunicatus vitandus,* violation of censures; [55] admission to ecclesiastical burial of such as are excluded by ecclesiastical law; [56] obduracy in censures; [57] violation of the law of enclosure; [58] usurpation of the goods and rights of the Roman Church; [59] usurpation and detention of temporal ecclesiastical goods and property; [60] illegal alienation of ecclesiastical goods; [61] unjust withholding of goods from pious institutes [62] and the refusal of legitimate contributions and taxes.[63]

Almost any delict can tend to contempt of the faith or of ecclesiastical authority if it is committed in certain aggravating circumstances. For an example one could point to an abortion performed by a Catholic doctor under the stress of grave fear if the fear was inflicted upon him to compel a practical admission that the teaching of the Church is of no consequence and hence is to be neglected. When an act tends thus to this special contempt, even though only by reason of circumstances, it must be included in this category.

[54] Canon 2335.

[55] Canon 2338, §§ 1, 2, 3; Claeys Bouuaert includes among the delicts which imply this special contempt the crime of knowingly admitting to the celebration of divine services those who are under censure. He adds the qualifying phrase "at least if this is done to belittle or ridicule the authority of the superior."—*art. cit.—Jus Pontificium,* VI (1926), 139. However, this last phrase shows that there is some doubt in his mind as to whether the objective crime taken in itself and in abstraction from such circumstances necessarily contains such contempt. Cf. also Michiels, *De Delictis et Poenis,* I, 211.

[56] Canon 2339.

[57] Canon 2340.

[58] Canon 2342.

[59] Canon 2345.

[60] Canon 2346.

[61] Canon 2347.

[62] Canon 2348.

[63] Canon 2349.

3. *Acts That Work To the Detriment of Souls*

These are all acts which draw people away from the faith or from the practice of Christian morals and thus expose them to the danger of eternal damnation.[64] This can be verified in view of the incidental circumstances in which the act is performed, for example, when scandal results or when sinful cooperation is present. It can also be such by the very nature of the act.[65] Those acts which by their nature work to the detriment of souls are listed particularly in Titles XVI and XVII of the Fifth Book of the Code. These Titles bear the headings: "Offenses committed in the Administration or Reception of Orders and of the Other Sacraments" and "Offenses Against the Obligations Proper to the Clerical and Religious State." Among the delicts listed here detriment to souls in the sense explained above seems objectively contained in the following delicts; in the administration of the sacraments to those who are forbidden to receive them;[66] in the attempt to administer Confirmation on the part of an unauthorized priest;[67] in the absolution of one's accomplice;[68] in the confessor's solicitation *ad turpia;*[69] in the failure of the penitent to denounce a priest who had made himself guilty of solicitation;[70] in the violation of the seal of confession;[71] in the consecration of a bishop without a papal mandate;[72] in simony regarding the administration or the reception of the sacraments;[73] in the reception of orders from unworthy prelates;[74] in the negligence of a pastor in care of souls[75]

[64] Cf. Roberti, *De Delictis et Poenis,* I, 153.

[65] Cf. Michiels, *De Delictis et Poenis,* I, 211-212.

[66] Canon 2364.

[67] Canon 2365.

[68] Canon 2367.

[69] Canon 2368, § 1.

[70] Canon 2368, § 2. This is evident, for the purpose of the obligation laid upon the solicited person is to prevent future harm to souls.

[71] Canon 2369.

[72] Canon 2370.

[73] Canon 2371.

[74] Canon 2372.

[75] Canon 2382.

and in the negligence in office on the part of the canon theologian and the canon penitentiary.[76]

The other delicts listed in Titles XVI and XVII do not seem to contain this special note of "detriment to souls." However, it should be noted that many of them may very easily involve such harm in certain circumstances, for example, the carelessness of a pastor in keeping the parochial records; [77] the neglect of residence when there is a shortage of priests or in other special dangers or necessities; [78] the discarding of the clerical garb [79] and the violation of the obligation of celibacy.[80] The latter two delicts often involve serious harm to souls because of scandal.

Article III. The Imputability of Delicts Committed Because of Necessity or Grave Hardship

Due to the fact that the canonical doctrine on force and fear in regard to imputability in penal matters has to a great extent grown out of the discussions among canonists regarding force and fear in contracts, the only fear considered under that term is fear from without *(ab extrinseco)*, such as is inflicted by a free human agent. Although fear from within, be it produced by an interior cause, e.g., sickness, or by a necessary exterior cause, is just as potent an excuse from imputability in delicts, its consideration has not been included in the doctrine on fear *ab extrinseco*. Canonists assign this fear to the category of necessity or grave hardship,[81] so *metus ab intrinseco* will also be included here under this category.

"Necessity renders licit what is not licit in the law." [82] Necessity and even grave hardship are considered as excusing causes parallel to grave fear. According to canon 2205, § 2, they also "as a rule" take away the delict completely when there is question

[76] Canon 2384.

[77] Canon 2383.

[78] Canon 2381.

[79] Canon 2379.

[80] Canon 2388.

[81] Cf. Wernz-Vidal, *Ius Canonicum*, VII, 107; Michiels, *De Delictis et Poenis*, I, 199-200.

[82] Reg. 4, X, *de Regulis Iuris*, V. 41.

of purely ecclesiastical laws.[83] And when an act is intrinsically evil, or involves contempt of the faith or of ecclesiastical authority, or works to the detriment of souls, then necessity and grave hardship, though not taking away the imputability of the delict, nevertheless diminish it to some extent.[84] Consequently the principles inculcated above in regard to the excusing effect of fear are to be applied likewise in the case of necessity or of grave hardship. To more fully understand the requisite conditions for a necessity or grave hardship to be a true excuse from imputability it is necessary to note the following.

When from a moral estimation the case of physical necessity or of grave hardship is connected with the observance of the law, it is first of all postulated that such a necessity or hardship be merely accidentally joined with the observance of the specific law, and not as something which is intended by the law or which naturally flows from the law. For every law and every obligation place some hardship upon the subject. Thus every restitution of stolen goods necessarily implies some hardship, some inconvenience.[85] Again, this necessity or hardship must be really grave or notable according to the common estimation of prudent men and the practice of the Church, and also in proportion to the gravity of the law. Finally, the harm or hardship must be inevitable apart from the violation of the law.[86] Such are the requirements regarding absolute necessity if it is to exist as an excuse from the penalty. However, necessity or hardship which is grave in relation to the person who suffers it seems likewise to be an excuse parallel to relatively grave fear.

[83] " . . . necessitas, imo et grave incommodum, plerumque delictum, si agatur de legibus mere ecclesiasticis, penitus tollunt."

[84] Canon 2205, § 3; "Si vero actus sit intrinsece malus aut vergat in contemptum fidei vel ecclesiasticae auctoritatis vel in animarum damnum, causae, de quibus in § 2, delicti imputabilitatem minuunt quidem, sed non auferunt."

[85] Cf. Van Hove, *Commentarium Lovaniense in Codicem Iuris Canonici,* Vol. I, Tom. II, *De Legibus Ecclesiasticis* (Mechliniae: H. Dessain, 1930), p. 298.

[86] Cf. Wernz-Vidal, *Ius Canonicum,* VII, 107-109; Michiels, *De Delictis et Poenis,* I, 206-207.

From a moral estimation an instance of spiritual necessity is had in the command of authority contrary to the existing penal law.[87] In such a case the following elements are postulated for constituting an excusing necessity. First, a real command, given in virtue of true authority recognized by law, and intimated to one who is actually a subject. This authority may be private or public. It must be presupposed, moreover, that the precept does not appear to the subject as manifestly illegitimate. This does not mean that the precept must be legitimate, but only that the subject be not aware of the manifest illegitimacy of the precept. For the norms of right government demand that the precepts of superiors be presumed legitimate. Their execution is ordinarily not to be subjected to the examination and judgment of the subject. But when a precept is manifestly, *prima facie,* illegitimate, then the subject is not to obey, for no one is to act against his own conscience. The subject would be acting against his own conscience if he were to carry out precepts contrary to the penal law if such precepts were evidently unjust or illegitimate.

A command given by the civil authority which is contrary to the existing merely human penal law must be considered as abrogating the existing law in this concrete case if the authority is competent in this respect.[88] Thus such a command evidently excuses an inferior of all criminal imputability in the matter. If the superior, however, excedes his authority by giving a command contrary to a law over which he has not the authority of dispensation, as for example the divine law, then the excuse, if any, will depend on the degree of responsibility which the law attaches to the individual inferior. This degree of responsibility may vary according to circumstances, e.g., in time of war.[89]

[87] Cf. Chelodi, *Ius Poenale,* p. 10; Wernz-Vidal, *Ius Canonicum,* VII, 110.

[88] Michiels, *De Delictis et Poenis,* I, 208. According to American Criminal Law there is no dispensing authority in civil superiors;—cf. Hall-Seligman, "*Mistake of Law and Mens Rea*"—University of Chicago Law Review, VIII (June, 1941), 641-682.

[89] American Criminal Law on this particular point is given in the *Corpus Iuris,* Vol. XVI, p. 91: "A crime is not excused on the ground of duress because it was committed . . . by an inferior in the army, navy or civil service, by command of his superior." This is based on a court deci-

When an ecclesiastical superior possessing true jurisdiction gives a command which contravenes a penal law, then all criminal imputability is taken away for an inferior, if the action commanded is within the sphere of the superior's power, and its malice be not altogether certain and evident to the subject. As regards the latter the subject cannot set himself up as a judge of the actions of the superior who is legally commanding. Thus the violation of the enclosure at the command of a legitimate superior ceases to be a crime,[90] and also the usurpation of ecclesiastical goods.[91] But if it is evident that the superior is exceeding his authority, then the imputability of the inferior's act remains intact, for in such a case he is not held to obey. There may be an excuse even in this latter case due to other causes, such as ignorance, fear, self-defense, etc.

Since a person with merely domestic authority or dominative power has no authority in matters of penal law, a command for example by a father to his son would not of itself exclude the imputability of the action of the son. However in practical specific cases there may often be an excuse because of grave fear, or inasmuch as the subject does not know the malice of the action.[92]

sion which contained the following dicta: "A soldier is bound to obey only the lawful orders of his superiors. If he receives an order to do an unlawful act he is bound neither by his duty nor his oath to do it. So far from such an order being a justification, it makes the party given the order an accomplice in the crime. For instance, an order from an officer to a soldier to shoot another for disrespectful words merely, if obeyed, would be murder, both in the officer and soldier." U. S. *vs.* Car. 25 F. Cas. No. 14, 732, I Woods 480, 483. This general rule is somewhat modified by a court of the state of Georgia. Here the inferior is liable under ordinary circumstances. (Hately *vs.* State, 15. Ga. 346.) But in time of war the orders of a superior have been held to be those of a despot and hence must be obeyed. In such circumstances the inferior is not liable. (Clark *vs.* State, 37. Ga. 191).

90 Canon 2342.

91 Canon 2346.

92 Cf. Michiels, *De Delictis et Poenis,* I, 207-208; Wernz-Vidal, *Ius Canonicum*, VII, 110-111; Latini, *Lineamenta*, pp. 125-126.

CHAPTER VI

THE EFFECTS OF FORCE AND FEAR UPON PENAL RESPONSIBILITY FOR *FERENDAE SENTENTIAE* PENALTIES

The preceding chapter dealt with the effects of force and fear upon delictual imputability in general. If it be kept in mind that there is a distinction between imputability and responsibility, and that not all delicts require the same degree of imputability, it will easily be seen that the general norms for imputability must be varied according to the nature of the crime and of the corresponding penalty to be imposed. In determining the sentence in a *ferendae sententiae* penalty, the judge has it for his duty to apply the general norms to each specific violation of the penal law.

Article I. The Influence of Force and Fear Upon *Dolus* and Perfect *Dolus*

The distinction between simple *dolus* and perfect *dolus* becomes elucidated through a clear consideration of canons 2200, § 1, and 2229, § 2. In the former canon *dolus* is defined as the deliberate will to violate the law. The condition of the will opposed to this is termed a "defect of liberty". Perfect *dolus,* though not expressly defined in the Code, is presupposed in canon 2229, § 2, and the state of the will which precludes such perfect *dolus* is described as "any diminution whatsoever of full deliberation on the part of the will." *Culpa,* as described above,[1] may be defined as a "voluntary neglect" either of obtaining the necessary knowledge or of employing the proper means to avert the harmful action.

There can be little doubt that force and fear have different effects upon the responsibility for the different classes of crimes which postulate a perfect *dolus,* a simple *dolus,* or merely a *culpa*. That a distinction must be made between simple *dolus* and perfect *dolus* in the case of *latae sententiae* penalties is clear from canon 2229, § 2. Since, however, this distinction is made by the Code only in reference to *latae sententiae* penalties, some canonists main-

[1] Cf. *supra,* p. 69.

tain that the distinction does not hold for *ferendae sententiae* penalties.[2] The majority of post-Code authors, however, adhere to the same distinction even for *ferendae sententiae* penalties.[3]

This seems logical, for the Code itself contains twenty instances in which *ferendae sententiae* penalties are enacted for crimes which according to canon 2229, § 2, would presuppose perfect *dolus.* For the expressions which in reference to *latae sententiae* penalties postulate full knowledge and deliberation (v. g. *praesumpserit, scienter)* are also used when the law imposes *ferendae sententiae* penalties.[4] Moreover, in some case both *ferendae* and *latae sententiae* penalties are enacted for crimes which postulate perfect *dolus.*[5]

These terms definitely received their technical meaning only at the time of the Constitution *Apostolicae Sedis* (1869),[6] which contained mainly *latae sententiae* penalties. If the Code now accepts this terminology also in some *ferendae sententiae* penalties, it is to be presumed that these terms retain the specific meaning given them in the Constitution *Apostolicae Sedis,* even though no explicit mention of this is made in regard to *ferendae sententiae* penalties. Looking just to the Code itself, one would expect uniformity of terminology in those laws which deal with the same subject, unless another meaning is specifically determined.[7]

When a law, therefore, postulates perfect *dolus,* all exterior force, vincible or invincible, fear, grave or slight, all true necessity and hardship exclude criminal responsibility for the penalty of the law as long as the materially criminal act was actually perpetrated in consequence of these causes. The reason is that these causes

[2] Roberti, *De Delictis et Poenis,* I, 276; Moersdorf, *Die Rechtssprache des Codex Juris Canonici,* pp. 374-375.

[3] E.g., Wernz-Vidal, *Ius Canonicum,* VII, 452; Vermeersch-Creusen, *Epitome,* III, nn. 521, 540; Beste, *Introductio in Codicem,* p. 953; Ayrinhac-Lydon, *Penal Legislation,* p. 174.

[4] Canons 2316; 2317; 2321; 2331, § 1; 2337, § 1; 2341; 2347; 2360, § 2; 2362; 2364; 2365; 2369, §§ 1, 2; 2371; 2391, § 2; 2399; 2406, § 1; 2412, 1°. Cf. Swoboda, *Ignorance,* p. 174, note 60.

[5] V. g., canons 2346; 2360; 2395. Cf. Swoboda, *loc. cit.*

[6] *Fontes,* n. 552.

[7] Cf. Swoboda, *Ignorance,* p. 174.

diminish imputability to a greater or lesser extent, and as a consequence that complete, full liberty which is postulated for perfect *dolus* is lacking.

If a law postulates *dolus* to the exclusion of a mere *delictum culposum,* then invincible physical force excuses from the penalty. This is the case even if one fell under such force through one's own negligence or imprudence. For in such an instance there is only *culpa,* not the *dolus* which postulates a deliberate will to commit the criminal action.[8]

Grave fear does not of necessity preclude simple *dolus,* since the deliberate will to violate the law can be present even when the agent is constrained to choose between a grave evil which is threatened and the actual violation of the law. The same must be said of vincible physical force, necessity and grave hardship. When the delinquent chooses to violate the law rather than to undergo the alternate evil, he deliberately chooses this as the lesser evil.

The law presumes *dolus* upon proof of the external violation of the penal law.[9] So the one alleging a positive fact such as the presence of invincible force as an excuse would have to prove the actual existence of such force. This seems to be the case also when there is question of those crimes which postulate perfect *dolus.* If one claims that the *dolus* was not perfect, but lessened because of some excusing factor, it seems to follow logically that the burden of proof rests upon the one who alleges this positive element. It would be assigning an impossible task to the accuser to require that he prove the negative fact, namely, the absence, for example, of grave fear. The truth is that this negative fact is often impossible to prove, since in the typical examples of ignorance or fear it is frequently known only to the accused himself. The purpose of the presumption with regard to simple *dolus* is evidently to prevent unscrupulous men from falsely alleging some such excuse as ignorance or fear.[10] The same reason is equally valid in

[8] Cf. Latini, *Lineamenta,* p. 131.

[9] Canon 2200, § 2.

[10] Cf. Vermeersch-Creusen, *Epitome,* III, n. 388. They state: "Favor enim callidis viris conciliaretur, si obi[i]cere ignorantiam iuris aut asserere se ioco vel ignorantia facti egisse sine probatione possent."

regard to those crimes which postulate perfect *dolus*.[11]

It would seem, then, that the chief difference between simple *dolus* and perfect *dolus* in regard to the matter of establishing by proof an excuse in the external forum consists not in any varied manner to be employed for proving that one or the other was not present, but rather in the varied facts which need to be proved. Thus a priest accused of unlawful bination is excused from the *ferendae sententiae* penalty of suspension from the celebration of Holy Mass,[12] if he can prove that he acted from even slight fear. Whereas, if canon 2321 had postulated only simple *dolus*, grave fear would have to be proved if he is to be held excused from the possible infliction of the penalty.[13] But in both cases the burden of proof would rest upon the one alleging this positive, excusing factor.

Article II. The Admission of Force and Fear in the External Forum

1. The Burden of Proof

The presumption of *dolus* as stated in canon 2200, § 2, does not give us an explicit presumption of the absence of grave fear when the external violation of the law is shown.[14] For grave fear does

[11] Swoboda (*Ignorance*, p. 175) has advanced the opinion that, since there is no explicit presumption of perfect *dolus*, given the proof of the objective violation of the law, in cases where perfect *dolus* is postulated for the punishment, the knowledge and will to place the prohibited act become objective characteristics of the crime and must be established by convincing evidence. He claims therefore that in such cases there must be proof not only that there was an objective violation of the law, but that the accused knowingly violated the law. Such an interpretation seems to contradict the fundamental norms of criminal procedure by demanding that the prosecution prove a negative fact such as the absence of fear or ignorance.

[12] Canon 2321.

[13] Although grave fear does not preclude *dolus*, it does "as a rule" excuse from all imputability if there is question of purely ecclesiastical laws, or if the acts are not intrinsically evil, do not involve contempt of the faith or of ecclesiastical authority, and do not work to the detriment of souls.—Canon 2205, §§ 2, 3.

[14] That the absence of invincible physical force is presumed in such cases is evident from the fact that such force and *dolus* cannot coexist in the same crime.

not necessarily preclude *dolus* and both can be found in the same violation of the criminal law. But the wording of canon 2218, § 2 shows that an excuse from grave fault in the commission of a delict must be proved in the external forum in order to free from punishment in this forum. *("si pro foro externo excusatio evincatur")*. Hence also in the case of grave fear as a factor diminishing the imputability, the burden of proof necessarily rests upon the accused. This is evident also from what has been said in the preceding article regarding the necessity of proving any positive, excusing cause.[15]

II. THE MANNER OF PROOF

Physical force, being of its nature external, is not so difficult to prove in the external forum. Fear, however, since it is essentially internal, is much more difficult to demonstrate. This difficulty is increased when there is question of *metus ab intrinseco,* which has been treated here under the heading of necessity and grave hardship. In all cases of alleged fear, great weight must be conceded to the testimony of the accused. Consequently the character of the accused and his reputation for veracity will have to be directly investigated. However, the mere word of the accused is never sufficient to establish proof of such an excusing fac-

[15] Sole *(De Delictis et Poenis,* p. 55) not distinguishing imputability from responsibility, makes the general statement that for one to be excused from any punishment either *ferendae* or *latae sententiae* in the external forum, a lack of grave imputability must be shown through legitimate proofs.

It is to be noted that the burden of proof rests upon the one alleging force or fear also in the parallel case of such force or fear in the marriage contract (canon 1087, § 1), in vows (canon 1307, § 3), in other contractual agreements (canon 103, § 2), also in exceptions and rescissory actions (canons 1698, § 1; 1684); Cf. Beste, *Introductio in Codicem,* pp. 157-158.

There is a rather interesting presumption of duress in secular criminal law. A wife who commits a crime in the presence of her husband is presumed to have done so because of duress from the husband. Some statutes, however, have changed this presumption. For example, section 1092 of the New York Penal Law states explicitly that it is not a defence to a married woman charged with crime that the alleged criminal act was committed by her in the presence of her husband—Sayre, *A Selection of Cases on Criminal Law* (Rochester, N. Y.: The Lawyers Co-Operative Publishing Company, 1927) pp. 462-464.

tor. His testimony must be corroborated by the deposition of others or by convincing external signs indicating the probability of the existence of such fear.[16]

As in other juridical proofs, two witnesses who are above suspicion and who testify to the existence of fear can establish proof of it beyond a doubt, even though there may be others who affirm complete liberty. This is the case because the one who testifies as to liberty speaks of something that is known only to God and can only be inferred from presumptions with a greater or lesser degree of certainty, whereas one who testifies to the existence of fear affirms something that can be known to the senses through certain external signs.[17] This does not imply that two witnesses are always required. Other supplementary proofs, such as external signs of fear, together with the assertion of the accused will at times be sufficient to establish the existence of fear.

III. THE SUPPLEMENTARY OATH IN CRIMINAL TRIALS

The question of the use of an oath by the accused to establish the presence of force or fear naturally arises in connection with the problem of demonstrating the presence of such force or fear as an excuse in the external forum. The use of an oath could seem to be of especial value in the case of alleged fear, since fear is an affection of the will known by experience only to the one suffering the fear. But canon 1830, § 2, seems rather clear in excluding the use of the oath by the accused in criminal trials. This is the interpretation generally given by the authors.[18]

[16] Similar testimony is required in proving fear in the matrimonial contract: Sipos, *Enchiridion,* p. 587; S.R.R., *Nullitatis Matrimonii,* 2 iul. 1918, *coram R.P.D. Petro Rossetti,* dec. VIII, nn. 4-6—*S.R.R. Dec.,* X (1918), 60-62; *AAS* XI (1919), 193-195.

[17] Cf. S.R.R., *Nullitatis Matrimonii,* 15 febr., 1919 *coram R.P.D. Guilelmo Sebastianelli, Decano,* dec. II, n. 2—*S.R.R. Dec.,* XI (1919), 10-11; *ASS,* XI (1919), 428-429.

[18] Cf. Vermeersch-Creusen, *Epitome,* III, n. 208; Beste, *Introductio in Codicem, p.* 809; *Moriarity (Oaths in Ecclesiastical Courts,* The Catholic University of America Canon Law Studies, n. 110 [Washington, D. C.: The Catholic University of America, 1937] p. 69) points out that the oath cannot be proffered either to the accused or to the promoter of justice.

Noval states that the reason for prohibiting the use of the oath by the accused in all criminal trials is the danger of perjury. If one admits this reason, such a danger must be said to be present in all criminal trials because all of them have a special gravity, concerning, as they do, the honor of a person.[19]

Still less can a judge in a criminal trial impose upon an accused a suppletory oath. Even apart from canon 1830 this is quite logical in view of the provisions of canons 1743, § 1, and 1744. According to the earlier of these canons no one is bound to answer questions concerning an offense committed by himself,[20] while canon 1744 states that the oath to tell the truth cannot be administered to the accused by the judge in criminal causes.[21]

[19] Cf. Noval, *De Processibus,* I, n. 568.

Swoboda *(Ignorance,* p. 188) admits the use of the suppletory oath. He argues from the grammatical construction of canon 1830, § 2, that the oath is forbidden only in those criminal cases which are specifically mentioned in the latter part of the paragraph. He also states that according to the traditional doctrine before the Code such a suppletory oath was allowed. But the grammatical construction of canon 1830, § 2, does not clearly indicate his contention that the clause beginning with *"si"* refers to both *causis criminalibus* and also to *causis contentiosis.* The canon reads: *"Sed eodem [iureiurando suppletorio] abstineat iudex tum in causis criminalibus, tum in contentiosis, si de iure vel re magni pretii agatur aut de facto nimii momenti, aut si ius, res, factum non sit proprium personae cui iusiurandum esset deferendum."* It is true that the *tum-tum* construction places both on an equal basis. But this does not necessarily imply that the modifying clause refers to both, especially in consideration of the subject matter, for of the three objects mentioned only one—*factum nimii momenti*—could refer to criminal trials, and this is mentioned in the third place. Besides, the condition that it regard a *factum nimii momenti* is always fulfilled in criminal trials, as explained above. As Moriarity points out *(Oaths in Ecclesiastical Courts,* p. 69), the doctrine of the pre-Code authors allowed a suppletory oath to be used in criminal trials of lesser moment in which the penalty inflicted in the event of condemnation was light, e.g., pecuniary fines. But since the Code makes no distinction between criminal trials of greater or minor importance, and all are considered of major importance, this opinion can no longer be accepted. Cf. Noval, *De Processibus,* n. 568; Reiffenstuel, lib. II, tit. XXIV, n. 49 (pre-Code opinion).

[20] "Iudici legitime interroganti partes respondere tenentur et fateri veritatem, nisi agatur de delicto ab ipsis commisso."

[21] "Iusiurandum de veritate dicenda in causis criminalibus nequit iudex accusato deferre."

Article III. The Rôle of Force and Fear in the Infliction of *Ferendae Sententiae* Penalties

The general principles of the penal imputability of crimes committed through force or fear considered together with the special requirements for *dolus* and perfect *dolus* are the necessary norms for ecclesiastical judges in deciding upon the infliction of a definite punishment in a specific instance of a violation of penal law. It devolves upon the judge to investigate in the individual case and to define by sentence that the criminal action has all the elements of a true delict punishable according to law; that the author of the criminal action placed it with that deliberation of mind and freedom of will required for imputability and consequent responsibility, or that there is some cause that precludes imputability or responsibility. Once the actual commision of the crime is proved, and the accused's imputability is evident, the judge is to estimate the degree of imputability according to the circumstances which are shown to increase or lessen it. Only after such considerations is the judge to give the sentence which inflicts the punishment. The punishment must be in conformity with the legitimate and special principles of penal law.[22] And so it will be useful to consider the application of the general norms of penal imputability to the question of *ferendae sententiae* penalties.

A fundamental canon for the interpretation of penal law is canon 2218, which insists on a just proportion between the punishment and the offense, and stresses the fact that attention must be paid to the various factors influencing the imputability. Grave fear is mentioned as one of these.[23] In the second paragraph of the same canon it is stated that not only those circumstances which excuse from all liability, but also those which excuse from grave imputability, excuse also from any *latae* or *ferendae sententiae* penalty even in the external forum, provided that the excuse is

[22] Cf. Wernz-Vidal, *Ius Canonicum,* VII, 189.

[23] "In poenis decernendis servetur aequa proportio cum delicto, habita ratione imputabilitatis . . . ; quare attendi debe(t) . . . num . . . ob gravem metum delinquens egerit."—canon 2218, § 1.

proved for this forum.[24] This is a general principle which must be applied also in the case of fear. Consequently, as often as fear lessens the *voluntarium* to such an extent that grave imputability and therefore grave guilt is lacking, the agent is not subject to any punishment.[25]

Canon 2205 is therefore to be explained in view of this clear principle of no punishment without grave imputability and grave guilt. The second paragraph of canon 2205 speaks of a delict "as a rule" being taken away by grave fear when there is question of merely ecclesiastical laws.[26] The canon in indicating possible exceptions by the word *plerumque* is evidently considering the case wherein the presence of grave fear does not preclude the presence of grave imputability. Such a situation is verified in the example of the administration of the sacraments to those who are infected with a contagious disease. If a rightful superior legitimately commands this, then grave fear would not free the act of omission from imputability in the case of disobedience. So also in the cases mentioned in the third paragraph of the same canon, those acts, namely, which are intrinsically evil, which involve contempt of the faith or of ecclesiastical authority, or which work to the detriment of souls. Grave fear does not excuse here as long as grave sin remains; but if the agent is so disturbed in mind that he sins only slightly, then the fear does excuse from incurring a penalty or also from having a penalty inflicted upon him.

The rules by which the judge or superior must be guided in the imposition of penalties are given in canon 2223. These will necessarily vary according to the wording of the penalty, namely whether it is determined by law or is merely indeterminate.

I. IN CASE OF A DETERMINED PENALTY

A law may state a determined penalty in facultative terms

[24] "Non solum quae ab omni imputabilitate excusant, sed etiam quae a gravi, excusant pariter a qualibet poena tum latae tum ferendae sententiae etiam in foro externo, si pro foro externo excusatio evincatur."—canon 2218, § 2. Cf. Sole, *De Delictis et Poenis,* p. 55.

[25] Cf. Claeys Bouuaert, *art. cit.—Jus Pontificium,* VI (1926), 140.

[26] "Metus quoque gravis . . . plerumque delictum, si agatur de legibus mere ecclesiasticis, penitus toll(it)."

(verba facultativa) or it may use words implying a precept *(verba praeceptiva)*. The rights and duties of the judge will vary according to this wording of the law.

1. A Penalty Determined in Falcultative Terms

When the law employs terms which leave an option to the judge, the inflicting of the penalty is thereby left to the discretion and conscience of the judge. In such an instance he may inflict the penalty or modify it according to his own good judgment.[27] Among the factors that he must consider before making a decision as to whether a penalty should be inflicted, and if so as to what amount of punishment ought to be imposed, are the excusing causes considered here, namely, force, both invincible and vincible, fear, both grave and slight, all true necessity and hardship. Some authors hold that slight fear is not to be considered in the external forum.[28] But slight fear must be recognized as a factor which can diminish imputability. This is evident from the very nature of such fear, since in all actions really done out of slight fear there is present an *involuntarium secundum quid.*[29]

2. A Penalty Determined in Preceptive Terms

If the law uses words implying a precept *(verba praeceptiva)* when it states a determined penalty, this is ordinarily to be imposed if the crime is imputable according to the general norms of delictual imputability.[30] But even in these cases the judge is given great latitude if there is a circumstance which diminishes the imputa-

[27] "Si lex in statuenda poena ferendae sententiae facultativis verbis utatur, committitur prudentiae et conscientiae iudicis eam infligere, vel, si poena fuerit determinata, temperare."canon 2223, § 2. Cf. Sipos, *Enchiridion,* p. 932; Chelodi, *Ius Poenale,* p. 22.

[28] E.g., Noldin-Schmitt, *Summa Theologiae Moralis,* I, *De Principiis* (23. ed., Oeniponte: Rauch, 1935), p. 65; Claeys Bouuaert, *art. cit.—Jus Pontificium,* VI (1926), 144.

[29] Noldin-Schmitt *(loc. cit.)* admit the influence of slight fear in the internal forum. Its rejection in the external forum is probably due to the influence of the law of contracts on this particular phase of penal law. Cf. *supra,* p. 39.

[30] Si vero lex utatur verbis praeceptivis, ordinarie poena infligenda est . . . "—canon 2223, § 3.

bility considerably. In such an instance he is at liberty to mitigate the punishment, or to give some penal remedy or penance as a substitute.[81] Consequently, in acts which are intrinsically evil, or which involve contempt of the faith or of ecclesiastical authority, or which work to the detriment of souls, grave fear, necessity and grave hardship do not excuse the delinquent from responsibility, but they do diminish the imputability of his delictual act.[82] If there is a considerable diminution of imputability in such instances, the judge can mitigate the punishment or substitute a penal remedy or penance. An example of this could occur in the crime of conspiracy against one's own ordinary. Grave fear, though not excusing from the penalties of canon 2331, § 2, would allow the judge to mitigate, for example, the penalty of loss of active and passive vote.

It should also be noted that whereas slight fear does not excuse from the violation of merely ecclesiastical laws, a slight fear which is just short of truly grave fear must be termed a circumstance which diminishes the imputability considerably, and thus allows the judge to mitigate the determined penalty. The same mitigation of punishment is possible in the similar case of slight necessity or hardship. In those instances wherein grave fear does not excuse from the violation of merely ecclesiastical laws, it will be an excusing factor diminishing the imputability considerably.[83]

II. IN CASE OF INDETERMINATE PENALTIES

When the law leaves it to the discretion of the judge to set the definite penalty, he is obliged to consider all the factors that increase or diminish imputability. Grave fear is explicitly mentioned as one of the factors that must be weighed in judgment. The fact that only "grave fear" is explicitly mentioned could seem to indicate that slight fear is not to be considered in the external

[81] "Poenam determinatam temperare vel loco ipsius aliquod remedium poenale adhibere aut aliquam poenitentiam iniungere, si detur circumstantia imputabilitatem notabiliter minuens . . . "—canon 2223, § 3, 3°.

[82] Canon 2205, § 3.

[83] Canon 2205, § 2.

forum.[84] And, in fact, some authors as already noted, evidently influenced by the discussion on fear in the matter of contracts, maintain that slight fear need not be considered by the judge in such cases.[85]

It has already been pointed out that slight fear, if it actually gives rise to the criminal deed, does diminish imputability, since it renders the act *involuntarium secundum quid,* no longer spontaneous. It must then be included among the factors to be weighed by the judge when he inflicts a penalty for a crime which carries an indeterminate penalty in law. Slight necessity and hardship are similarly excusing factors. The difficulty of establishing proof of the existence of these factors in the external forum is evident. But this does not argue against their value as excuses when their existence has been duly proved.

[84] Canon 2218, § 1.

[85] E.g., Wernz-Vidal, *Ius Canonicum,* VII, 104; Noldin-Schmitt, *De Principiis,* p. 65; Claeys Bouuaert, *art. cit.—Jus Pontificium,* VI (1926), 144.

CHAPTER VII

THE EFFECTS OF FORCE AND FEAR UPON PENAL RESPONSIBILITY FOR *LATAE SENTENTIAE* PENALTIES

Article I. Observations on Canon 2229

In the preceding chapter the norms for a judge or superior in inflicting *ferendae sententiae* penalties were noted. Much is left to the discretion and conscience of the judge. He is to adapt the penalty to the specific criminal violation, taking into account the various factors that influence subjective responsibility. In canon 2229 the Code gives a detailed set of rules regarding the causes which excuse from *latae sententiae* penalties in view of the lessening of subjective responsibility. It is to be expected that the law would be more specific here, since there is no judge to weigh the various factors and apply the penalties. Here the individual must decide for himself whether or not he has incurred the penalty. The rules of general imputability for delictual acts in the case of force or fear as determined in canon 2205 are somewhat modified here in their application to *latae sententiae* penalties.

As noted in the historical synopsis of the present work,[1] pre-Code authors were clear in stating that whatever excused from grave fault excused also from grave censures, and whatever excused from a delict, or even only from contumacy, excused likewise from grave censures.[2] But there was some dispute as to just what constituted an excuse from a delict or from contumacy. They commonly taught that even relatively grave fear excused from all penalties when there was question of purely ecclesiastical laws. But it was disputed whether grave fear excused in case the laws were not merely ecclesiastical laws, i.e., when the acts were forbidden concomitantly by the divine natural or positive law. Those who held that grave fear excused in such instances placed certain exceptions to this rule. Thus they pointed out that grave fear did not excuse when the observance of the law, even though it was

[1] Cf. *supra*, p. 47.

[2] Cf., e.g., Ojetti, *Synopsis*, s.v. *censura*, n. 965.

a human law, was judged necessary for the protection of the public good, or when its violation would involve contempt of the faith, of the law or of ecclesiastical power.[8]

In canon 2229 appears the first express and universal legislation on this subject. This canon was evidently meant to settle the points of law mentioned above as doubtful and disputed at the time of the codification. It was meant to regulate and to determine the excusing effects of those causes which affect the imputability of delictual acts either on the part of the intellect or on the part of the will in relation to the concept of perfect *dolus,* and these excusing effects are now clearly defined. It was meant to accomplish this task in relation to vindictive and medicinal penalties, and all the pertinent elements are now clearly distinguished. As is to be expected in such a subject, there are many questions and possibilities in relation to force and fear which are not clearly expressed here. These are left to be determined according to the general principles of delictual imputability and penal responsibility and the common doctrine of the canonists in the light of the present legislation.

The same rules which regard fear as an excusing cause apply equally to vindictive and medicinal penalties. Canon 2229 draws its main distinction not from the nature of the penalty but from the nature of the crime, namely, whether the crime postulates perfect *dolus,* or whether simple *dolus* or even *culpa* is sufficient to beget the incurring of a penalty for a delictual act.

ARTICLE II. *Latae Sententiae* PENALTIES FOR CRIMES POSTULATING PERFECT *Dolus*

In canon 2229, § 2, which regulates *latae sententiae* penalties for delicts which postulate perfect *dolus,* there is contained the first express statement to the effect that the laws containing the words "*praesumpserit, consulto egerit,* etc." require also full freedom on the part of the will. Pre-Code authors usually referred

[8] Cf., e.g., Reiffenstuel, lib. V, tit. XXXIX, n. 34; Schmalzgrueber, lib. V, tit. XXXIX, n. 79. Ballerini-Palmieri (*Opus Theologicum Morale,* VII, n. 159) stated that the opinion maintaining that grave fear excused even in case of an intrinsically evil act, with the exceptions noted above, was the common, if not also the universal opinion.

only to full knowledge as the requisite in such instances.[4] Although, as Crnica shows,[5] some of the writers after the Constitution *Apostolicae Sedis* (1869) [6] did consider that absolute freedom of will was also necessary when the law contained the terms *temerarie, consulto egerit*, etc.[7]

I. Force

1. *Invincible Physical Force*

Since canon 2205, § 1, entirely precludes a delict in the case of physical force which cannot be resisted, it follows logically that there can be no question of any penalty when the agent is thus compelled to the material violation of the penal law, especially when this law postulates perfect *dolus*.

2. *Vincible Physical Force*

Although not expressly mentioned in either canon 2205 or canon 2229, this force certainly must be recognized as diminishing imputability. Such vincible force may be either grave or slight according as a greater or lesser hardship is involved. And both slight and grave vincible force must be admitted as excusing from the incurring of those *latae sententiae penalties* in which the law postulates perfect *dolus*, whenever the criminal act is really performed under the influence of such force.

[4] Cf., e.g., St. Alphonsus (1696-1787), *Theologia Moralis*, lib. VII, nn. 45-47; D'Annibale (1815-1892), *Summula Theologiae Moralis*, lib. I, n. 312; Wernz (1842-1914), *Ius Decretalium*, VI, n. 158; Claeys Bouuaert, "De metus influxu quoad valorem actuum et quoad delicta et poenas secundum Codicem Juris Canonici,"—*Jus Pontificium*, VI (1926), 141.

[5] "De metu gravi ut causa eximente a poenis latae sententiae,"—*Jus Pontificium*, V (1925), 11.

[6] *Fontes*, n. 552. This Constitution of Pius IX (1846-1878) substituted certain excommunications for those whose enactment had been contained in the bull *"Coenae"* and, what is of importance in this connection, added to certain delicts a special clause concerning *"scientia"* and *"audacia"* as being postulated for the incurring of the penalty. This is what led the authors to conclude, and rightly so, that even slight fear excused from *latae sententiae* censures if one of these special clauses was contained in a law.—Cf. Crnica, *art. cit.*,—*Jus Pontificium* V (1925), 11.

[7] Cf. e.g., Santi (1830-1885)—Leitner (1862-1929), *Praelectiones Iuris Canonici*, V, pp. 192-193 n. 13.

II. FEAR AS AN EXCUSE FROM *Latae Sententiae* PENALTIES WHEN PERFECT *Dolus* IS POSTULATED

1. Grave Fear

There can be no dispute as to the fact that grave fear is included among the causes that generally excuse from the incurring of *latae sententiae* penalties when perfect *dolus* is postulated by the penal law. For when grave fear is present there is undoubtedly a diminution of responsibility on the part of the will. Thus grave fear certainly excuses from the penalty enacted for those who presume in their non-possession of the proper faculty to absolve from a *latae sententiae* excommunication when absolution from it is reserved in a most special or also in a special manner to the Apostolic See.[8] Such fear would likewise excuse from incurring the penalties enacted for participation with an *excommunicatus vitandus* in the crime on account of which he was excommunicated, and for the violation of the prohibitions resultant upon a local interdict or consequent to a censured status in clerics.[9] Grave fear would also excuse from the liability for *latae sententiae* penalties as determined for the violation of the obligation of celibacy.[10]

Canonists dispute as to whether this grave fear also excuses when perfect *dolus* is postulated, even if the delict involves contempt of the faith, or of ecclesiastical authority, or works to the public injury of souls. The text of canon 2229 clearly distinguishes between the cases wherein perfect *dolus* is postulated *("Si lex habeat verba")* and wherein simple *dolus* or *culpa* is sufficient *("Si lex verba illa non habeat")*. And only in the latter case does it assert that grave fear does not excuse from *latae sententiae* penalties if the crime involves contempt of the faith, etc. In view of this evident textual argument it seems clear that grave fear does excuse at all times if perfect *dolus* is required. And this is

[8] Canon 2338, § 1.

[9] Canon 2338, §§ 2, 3.

[10] Canon 2388.

the explicit teaching of many of the authors.[11] However, there are some canonists who hold that grave fear does not excuse from *latae sententiae* penalties in such instances. Cappello has advanced a number of arguments in defense of this opinion.[12] It is well here to note the various arguments adduced by Cappello in order that the reader may obtain a better understanding of the controversy.

First, in order to show that he does not stand alone in his opinion, Cappello cites quite a number of the leading canonists and moralists as holding the same view.[13] These authors in commenting on canon 2229, § 3, seem to state that grave fear would never excuse from *latae sententiae* penalties when contempt of the faith etc. is involved in the criminal act. But it should be remarked that most of the authors mentioned are not formally treating the question involved here. They are commenting on the Code and following the order of the canon. Thus, after having explained canon 2229, § 2, under the heading *"Si lex habeat verba praesumpserit etc."*, and having stated that any diminution of liberty is enough to excuse in such cases, they proceed to explain canon 2229, § 3, under the heading *"Si lex verba illa non habeat."* Cappello quotes their comments on this latter section as supporting his opinion. Thus he quotes Noldin-Schönegger: *"Metus gravis, si delictum vergat in contemptum fidei etc. . . . a poenis latae sententiae nullatenus eximit* (c. 2229, § 2, 3°). *In his enim casibus metus gravis neque ab observanda lege ecclesiastica excusat."* [14]

[11] Cf., e.g., Cocchi,*Commentarium in Codicem Iuris Canonici,* (5 vols. in 8, 1922-1930), Lib. V, *De Delictis et Poenis* (Taurinorum Augustae: Marietti, 1925), p. 75; Sipos, *Enchiridion,* p. 934; Ayrinhac-Lydon, *Penal Legislation,* p. 60; Claeys Bouuaert, *art. cit.,—Jus Pontificium,* VI (1926), 141-144; Crnica, *art. cit.,—Jus Pontificium,* V (1925), 10-15.

[12] He first advanced this opinion in his work on censures, *De Censuris Iuxta Codicem Iuris Canonici,* p. 21, and later defended this position in an article in the *Jus Pontificium* ("Tres Quaestiones circa Censuras", *Jus Pontificium,* V [1925], 129-132).

[13] E.g., Noldin (1838-1922)—Schönegger, *De Censuris* (28. ed., Oeniponte: Rauch, 1935), n. 26; Vermeersch (1858-1936)—Creusen, *Epitome,* III, n. 423; Cipollini, *De Censuris Latae Sententiae iuxta Codicem Iuris Canonici* (Taurini: Marietti, 1925) p. 22.

[14] *De Censuris,* n. 26.

But Noldin-Schönegger plainly preface this with the words "*si lex verba non habeat.*" In treating of paragraph 2 of canon 2229 they state that any diminution of knowledge or of liberty excuses, and they mention only affected ignorance either of law or even of the punishment alone as the sole exception.[15]

In his second argument, Cappello appeals to the opinion of the pre-Code authors, citing Reiffenstuel (1641-1703)[16] and Suarez (1548-1617)[17] as representing this doctrine. But, as was pointed out above,[18] up to the time of the Constitution *Apostolicae Sedis* (1869) the terms *praesumpserit etc.* had no fixed meaning in law. They were usually employed to stress the objective gravity of the crime rather than the special degree of subjective responsibility postulated for the incuring of the penalty.[19] Even after this Constitution of Pius IX (1846-1878), many pre-Code authors gave explicit consideration only to the factor of the lack of full knowledge as occasioning an excuse from the penalty when perfect *dolus* was postulated in the penal law. These authors did not exclude grave fear as an excusing factor, but rather just did not explicitly consider the problem. This was quite natural inasmuch as canon 2229, § 2 is actually the first instance in ecclesiastical law whereby full freedom of the will is designated as a prerequisite condition for the incurring of the penalty whenever the penal law postulates the presence of perfect *dolus* in the criminal act.[20] However, as Crnica recalls, there were some among the later authors, especially among those who wrote after the issuance of the Constitution

[15] Vermeersch-Creusen (*Epitome,* III, n. 423), although explaining the canon in a manner similar to Noldin-Schönegger, point to canon 2369, § 1, which deals with the direct violation of the seal of confession, as an example of an instance in which *metus gravis* would not excuse. Since this canon postulates perfect *dolus* for the incurring of the penalty *("qui sigillum sacramentale directe violare praesumpserit"),* Vermeersch-Creusen do seem to favor the opinion of Cappello. Roberti *(De Delictis et Poenis,* I, 278) gives similar examples.

[16] Lib. V, tit. XXXIX, n. 34.

[17] *De Censuris—Opera Omnia,* Tom. XXIII, disp. IV, sect. 3, n. 13.

[18] Cf. *supra,* p. 51.

[19] Cf. Hollweck (1854-1926), *Die kirchlichen Strafgesetze,* pp. 96-97, § 29, note 3; Kuttner, *Schuldlehre,* pp. 74-76; Swoboda, *Ignorance,* p. 94.

[20] Claeys Bouuaert, *art. cit.,—Jus Pontificium,* VI (1926), 141.

Apostolicae Sedis, who did point out that even slight fear would excuse when perfect *dolus* was postulated for giving rise to the penalty. But none of these considered the precise question under discussion here. And, as is evident, this question which arose only after the Constitution *Apostolicae Sedis* cannot be solved with an appeal to opinions which flourished before that time.[21]

Cappello argues that the foundation for the incurring of a censure is the same in the Code as in the previous law. He points out that the principle of older commentators, which held that "grave fear excuses from punishments only in so far as it exempts from observing the law and therefore takes away the imputability of the crime," is now found re-expressed in canon 2205, § 3.[22] But, though even an identity of terminology with the older canonists in their explanation of this principle be admitted, it must simultaneously be stressed that the question is one which simply regards the general principle of imputability, which principle gives way to the more specialized rule for responsibility, as found in canon 2229, § 2. That the general principle of canon 2205, § 3, is modified by canon 2229 is evident from the response of the Pontifical Commission for the Interpretation of the Code, given December 30, 1937, in reference to canon 2229, § 3. This response states that grave fear excuses from *latae sententiae* penalties even though the delict be intrinsically evil and gravely culpable, provided that it does not involve contempt of the faith, or of ecclesiastical authority, or work to the public harm to souls.[23]

The fact that the word "delict" is used in canon 2205, § 3,[24] is stressed by Cappello to show that the punishment for such offenses is never taken away, since a delict according to canon 2195 always implies at least an indeterminate penalty. But the term "delict" in canon 2205, § 3, must be taken in a broader sense than that which it has in canon 2195, § 1. It evidently denotes some violation or fault which is imputable regardless of any canonical

[21] Crnica, *art. cit.,—Jus Pontificium,* V (1925), 11.

[22] *Art. cit.,—Jus Pontificium,* V (1925), 131.

[23] *AAS,* XXX (1938), 73.

[24] "Si vero actus sit intrinsece malus, aut vergat in contemptum . . . [metus gravis] delicti imputabilitatem . . . non [aufert]."

sanction. This is evident from the response of the Pontifical Commission mentioned just above.[25] From this it is seen that the term "delict" in canon 2205, § 3, cannot be taken strictly in the sense of a violation "to which at least an indeterminate canonical sanction is added,"[26] for the *latae sententiae* penalty is taken away by grave fear in the case of intrinsically evil acts, even though such acts are clearly imputable according to canon 2205, § 3.

In view of the clarity of the text of the canon it seems that one cannot argue from the discussion that took place at the time of the codification. Cappello asserts that various documents of the codification show that the legislator did not want to change the existing doctrine on this point.[27] But the discussions were secret, and hence nothing certain can be drawn from the schema. On the other hand, the law as it now stands in the text of the Code is very clear. Claeys Bouuaert gives as the reason why the law should so read, the desire on the part of the legislator to extend to the factor of grave fear a strength similar to that already enjoyed by gravely culpable ignorance in those canons which incorporate the words *praesumpserit*, etc.[28]

From the above considerations it is logical to conclude that the doctrine defended here is not really doubtful. Otherwise one would be introducing a limitation which is in no wise proved or corroborated by the text of canon 2229, § 2: "Any lessening of liability . . . on the part of the will excuses from *latae sententiae* penalties." Cappello claims that the matter is doubtful. Maintaining that the doubt concerns whether or not the new law differs from the old law, which latter he says is certain, he applies canon 6, 4°,[29] to indicate that one may not depart from the interpretation of the old law. But, even if one admitted that the present law is doubtful, one would have to insist that the old law was also doubtful in this particular point, since the question was not ex-

[25] *AAS,* XXX (1938), 73. Cf. Roberti's commentary on this response in *Apollinaris,* XI (1938), 180.

[26] Canon 2195, § 1.

[27] *Art. cit.,—Jus Pontificium,* V (1925), 132.

[28] *Art. cit.,—Jus Pontificium,* VI (1926), 144.

[29] "In dubio num aliquod canonum praescriptum cum veteri iure discrepet, a veteri iure non est recedendum."

plicitly discussed after the Constitution *Apostolicae Sedis* (1869),[30] when the terms *praesumpserit, temerarie,* etc. attained their present specific meaning.[31] So in this case canon 19 would have to be applied. This canon states that laws which enact penalties are to be strictly interpreted from the viewpoint of what the law demands. And canon 2219, § 1, calls for the more favorable interpretation in punishments from the viewpoint of the potential delinquent.[32]

Thus grave fear excuses from the punishment determined for parents who offer their children to non-Catholic ministers for baptism, or who educate and rear them in a non-Catholic religion,[33] and grave fear likewise excuses from the excommunication which is enacted for knowingly selling, distributing or exposing false relics.[34] Such fear, then, moreover excuses from the excommunication which derives from a penitent's failure to denounce the confessor who made himself guilty of solicitation,[35] and from the penalties enacted for presuming to administer Confirmation beyond the limits of one's faculties,[36] for hearing confessions without faculties,[37] for any direct violation of the seal of confession,[38] for receiving orders from unworthy prelates,[39] for simoniacally administering or receiving the sacraments,[40] for ordering or forcing ecclesiastical burial in violation of the prohibiton of canon 1240, § 1,[41] and for the violation of the privilege of the ecclesiastical forum.[42]

[30] Crnica, *art. cit.,—Jus Pontificium,* V (1925), 11.

[31] Cf. *supra,* p. 51.

[32] Joseph Glaser *(Pastoral-Fälle,"*—LQS, LXXXIII [1930], 120-125) adds that if number 3 of paragraph 3 in canon 2229 were not to be understood as strictly included under the heading at the beginning of the paragraph ("Si lex verba illa non habeat;") there would have to be some restricting clause placed in this number 3, such as is found in paragraph 1 ("licet lex verba de quibus in § 2 contineat").

[33] Canon 2319, § 1, 3°, 4°.

[34] Canon 2326.

[35] Canon 2368, § 2.

[36] Canon 2365.

[37] Canon 2366.

[38] Canon 2369, § 1.

[39] Canon 2372.

[40] Canon 2371.

[41] Canon 2339.

[42] Canon 2341.

Grave fear likewise excuses from the *latae sententiae* penalty attaching to the crimes which involve harm to souls, even when this is public, provided that the penal law postulates perfect *dolus.*

2. Slight Fears as an Excuse from *Latae Sententiae* Penalties when Perfect *Dolus* is Postulated.

Although many canonists still maintain that slight fear never excuses from a penalty,[43] it seems that according to the wording of canon 2229, § 2 ("any diminution of imputability . . . with regard to the will"), slight fear does excuse from *latae sententiae* penalties when the law postulates perfect *dolus.* It could be argued that this phrase must be understood with reference to canon 2205, wherein the causes of force and fear as diminishing liability are listed, and wherein nevertheless only *metus gravis,* and not *metus levis,* is mentioned. However, as shown above,[44] the list given in canon 2205 is not an exhaustive one. It must be conceded that when the criminal act is performed under the influence of a slight fear there is present an *involuntarium secundum quid* which correspondingly effects a lessening of the imputability. So much for the psychological aspects of this problem.

From the standpoint of canonical doctrine is it correct to assert, as does Claeys Bouuaert,[45] that to admit slight fear as an excuse from the incurring of penalties is to contravene all canonical tradition? It is true that until the Constitution *Apostolicae Sedis* (1869) *metus levis* was never considered as sufficing to excuse from *latae sententiae* penalties. But it was certainly considered a factor capable of effecting some diminution of imputability.[46] The fact that it never excused from *latae sententiae* penalties is easily explained by the fact that the terms *praesumpserit, consulto*

[43] E.g., Claeys Bouuaert, *art. cit.,—Jus Pontificium,* VI (1926), 144; Cavigioli, *De Censuris Latae Sententiae quae in Cadice Juris Canonici Continentur Commentariolum* (Torino, 1918), p. 27, n. 32 (hereafter cited *De Censuris).*

[44] Cf. *supra,* pp. 90, 111-113.

[45] *Art. cit.,—Jus Pontificium,* VI (1926), 144.

[46] Cf., e.g., Laymann (1575-1635), *Theologia Moralis,* lib. III, tract. IV, cap. VI, n. 5; Schmalzgrueber (1663-1735), lib. I, tit. XL, n. 23; *supra,* p. 43.

egerit, etc., which now postulate perfect *dolus*, were not determined in this specific meaning until that time.[47] Although many canonists after the Constitution *Apostolicae Sedis* still treated the question of perfect *dolus* only from the single consideration of perfect knowledge, and not with relation to the further consideration of full deliberation of the will,[48] among those who did recognize perfect *dolus* as postulating a complete and full freedom of the will were some who admitted slight fear as an excusing cause in respect of *latae sententiae* penalties when the law contained the expressions *temerarie, consulto egerit, studiose*, etc.[49]

The opinion that slight fear excuses from the *latae sententiae* penalty when the law postulates perfect *dolus* is quite common among the authors who have written since the Code.[50] It has already been shown that grave fear excuses in delicts which postulate perfect *dolus* when these delicts entail contempt of the faith, or of ecclesiastical authority, or work to the public harm to souls. It seems to follow logically that slight fear, once it is admitted as capable of diminishing liability, also excuses in the same cases. Some of the authors, however, disavow this conclusion. Claeys Bouuaert, who defends the opinion that grave fear excuses in these cases, eliminates the present question by excluding slight fear altogether as an excusing cause even when perfect *dolus* is postulated for the delictual violation of the penal law in question.[51]

Crnica [52] though admitting slight fear as an excuse which obtains ordinarily when perfect *dolus* is postulated, denies that it excuses if the delict tends to a contempt of the faith, etc. He argues from the fact that grave fear alone is mentioned in paragraph 3, number 3, of canon 2229.[53] He says that slight fear does

[47] Cf. *supra*, pp. 51-52.

[48] Cf. *supra*, p. 52.

[49] Cf. Crnica, *art. cit.,—Jus Pontificium*, V (1925), 11.

[50] Cf., e.g., Cocchi *De Delictis et Poenis*, p. 75; Ayrinhac-Lydon, *Penal Legislation*, p. 41; Cappello, *De Censuris*, p. 21; Crnica, *art. cit.,—Jus Pontificium*, V (1925), 14; Cerato, *Censurae Vigentes*, p. 52.

[51] *Art. cit.,—Jus Pontificium*, VI (1926), 144.

[52] *Art. cit.,—Jus Pontificium*, V (1925), 14.

[53] "Metus gravis, si delictum vergat in contemptum fidei . . . nullatenus eximit."

not excuse from *latae sententiae* penalties in these cases although the contrary may seem deducible from canon 2229, § 2. The reason he gives is that paragraph 3 makes exceptions for these delicts. The canon here states that if the law does not embody the restrictive wording, then grave fear in no wise excuses from *latae sententiae* penalties if the delict tends to a contempt of faith, etc. He concludes that if the law does have these words, then grave fear does excuse from *latae sententiae* penalties if the delict tends to a contempt of the faith, etc., i.e., grave fear only, but not slight fear.[54]

This argument does not appear conclusive. The solution for the cases in which perfect *dolus* is postulated is already given exclusively in paragraph 2 of canon 2229. This is clear in itself, and in no way demands an explanation from a parallel place.[55] Besides, it should appear evident that paragraph 3, number 3, of canon 2229, does not need to make mention of slight fear for the simple reason that in this case it would not excuse *a fortiori*. Crnica's argument fails against the rule that two negative premises yield no conclusion.

It seems eminently logical, therefore to hold that slight fear does excuse in enacted delicts which postulate perfect *dolus* even when these delicts entail a contempt of the faith or of ecclesiastical authority, or work to the public harm to souls. But it must be stressed that slight fear excuses from the *latae sententiae* penalty only when it really influences the criminal act. Thus, for example, slight fear excuses from the *latae sententiae* excommunication reserved to the ordinary for the crime of offering one's children to non-Catholic ministers for baptism, or for having one's children educated or reared in a non-Catholic religion.[56]

III. NECESSITY AND HARDSHIP AS EXCUSES FROM *Latae Sententiae* PENALTIES WHEN PERFECT *Dolus* IS POSTULATED

Paralleling fear as an excuse from penalties are necessity and grave hardship. These are placed upon a level with grave fear

[54] *Art. cit.,—Jus Pontificium,* V (1925) 14; also Cerato, *Censurae Vigentes,* p. 52.

[55] Cf. Claeys Bouuaert, *art. cit.,—Jus Pontificium,* VI (1926), 144, note 1.

[56] Canon 2319, § 1, 3°, 4°.

as excluding or diminishing the imputability of a delict.[57] Consequently they must be numbered among the causes that are referred to in canon 2229, § 2, for in case either of necessity or of grave hardship there is certainly a "lessening of liability or imputability with regard to the will." These, then, excuse whenever the law postulates perfect *dolus,* even when the delict tends to a contempt of the faith, etc., as has been maintained above in regard to fear.

Just as slight fear has been shown to be an excuse from *latae sententiae* penalties when perfect *dolus* must be presupposed as present before the delictual act can ensue, so also slight necessity and slight hardship excuse if they really influence the act in such a way as to make it an *involuntarium secundum quid,* so that it is no longer spontaneous. If this latter condition is verified, then there is a diminution of liability on the part of the will similar to that which accompanies acts performed *ex metu levi.*

Article III. *Latae Sententiae* Penalties for Crimes Postulating *Dolus* to the Exclusion of Mere *Culpa*

As explained above,[58] some delicts, while not postulating perfect *dolus,* do by their very definition or by the express will of the legislator imply the prerequisite of *dolus* to the exclusion of implying merely the presence of *culpa.* Among the excusing causes considered here, there is one—invincible physical force—which always excludes the presence of *dolus.* Such force, when it really gives rise to the action, necessarily excludes "a deliberate will to violate the law," such as is required for the very existence of *dolus.*[59]

A clear example of a delict that postulates *dolus* is the delict of procuring an abortion.[60] The expression *procurantes* shows that

[57] Canon 2205, § 2.

[58] Cf. *supra,* p. 67.

[59] Canon 2200, § 1.

[60] Canon 2350, § 1. Cf. Roberti, *De Delictis et Poenis,* I, 277; Cappello, *De Censuris,* p. 334. Eichmann, who apparently does not distinguish between perfect *dolus* and simple *dolus,* lists the term *"procurare"* as postulating the kind of *dolus* which is spoken of in canon 2229, § 2.—*Das Strafrecht Des Codex Iuris Canonici,* p. 69. For a complete explanation of the

there is required a direct will for the commission of the act and that consequently the delict cannot be committed through mere negligence. Now, in the case of invincible physical force there may be negligence in not avoiding the particular circumstances in which one would be subjected to such force. But then there is not present the true *dolus* which the law postulates for the commission of the delict of abortion as mentioned in canon 2350, § 1. And so, in case of invincible physical force, the woman, for instance, never incurs the *latae sententiae* penalty of excommunication reserved to the ordinary even when there has been *culpa* on her part.

Grave fear, necessity and grave hardship do not necessarily preclude *dolus*. Consequently their excusing effect will be the same for delicts which postulate *dolus* as for those in which *culpa* suffices to occasion the incurring of the penalty.

ARTICLE IV. *Latae Sententiae* PENALTIES FOR CRIMES IN WHICH EITHER *Dolus* OR *Culpa* IS SUFFICIENT

I. FORCE AS AN EXCUSE IN SUCH CRIMES

Canon 2205, § 1, states that absolute physical force excuses completely from liability. Consequently, since a materially criminal action committed under stress of such force is not imputable, it cannot become a basis for the incurring of any punishment either *ferendae sententiae* or *latae sententiae*. This presupposes there has been neither culpable negligence nor imprudence on the part of the one suffering the force.

Vincible physical force may be classified either as necessity or as hardship, and excuses to the same degree that these causes excuse in crimes for which either *dolus* or *culpa* suffice.

II. FEAR AS AN EXCUSE IN SUCH CRIMES

1. Grave Fear

According to canon 2229, § 3, 3°, if a law does not postulate

term "*procurare*" in reference to abortion see Huser, *The Crime of Abortion in Canon Law*, The Catholic University of America Canon Law Studies, No. 162 (Washington, D. C.: The Catholic University of America Press, 1942), pp. 81-88.

perfect *dolus,* then grave fear does not exempt from *latae sententiae* penalties if the offense entails a contempt of the faith or of ecclesiastical authority, or begets a public injury to souls. The logical conclusion is, therefore, that grave fear does exempt from *latae sententiae* penalties if the delict does not entail such a contempt of the faith, etc. The reason for this is that the agent is considered as acting from frailty rather than through obstinacy. Cipollini states that although the obligation of the natural law remains in some instances, the obligation of the ecclesiastical law regarding penalties ceases.[61]

It should be noted that the cases wherein grave fear exempts from *latae sententiae* penalties are considerably more extensive than the cases wherein it simply takes away all delictual imputability. Canon 2205, § 3, mentions that the imputability is not taken away if the act is intrinsically evil; this canon moreover, does not contain the modifier "public" in connection with *animarum damnum.*[62] But from canon 2229, § 3, 3°, one can infer that grave fear exempts from *latae sententiae* penalties even if the act is intrinsically evil, and that the harm to souls must be public to exclude grave fear as an excuse.[63] Hence even though the crime of procuring an abortion,[64] which is intrinsically evil, is imputable when done under grave fear, it does not furnish a basis for the incurring of the *latae sententiae* penalty of excommunication reserved to the ordinary. And so in regard to homicide, fornication, theft and blasphemy,[65] grave fear exempts from whatever *latae sententiae* penalty may be attached to the crime.

The term "public" is evidently used in canon 2229, § 3, 3°, as opposed to "occult", and not in opposition to "private". For, as Wernz-Vidal point out, harm to souls is never considered a private

[61] *De Censuris Latae Sententiae,* p. 22.

[62] Cf. Roberti's commentary on the response of the Pontifical Commission in this matter—*Apollinaris,* XI (1938), 180-181.

[63] Cf. response from the Pontifical Commission for the Authentic Interpretation of the Code, December 30, 1937—*AAS,* XXX (1938), 73.

[64] Canon 2350, § 1.

[65] Canon 2323.

matter in the Church.[66] When, then, would such harm to souls not be occult? Since there is question of *latae sententiae* penalties, that is, such as are incurred at the time the crime is committed, only that case wherein the harm is public at the time of the actual commission of the criminal act can be considered here. Otherwise the delinquent would be uncertain as to the incurring of the penalty until the harm became public, or until it became certain that it would remain occult. Using canon 2197 as a guide one can maintain that the harm to souls is public in the sense spoken of in canon 2229, § 3, 3°, whenever the crime which evidently entails injury to souls is committed under such circumstances that it is immediately divulged or that it may and must be prudently considered that it easily will be divulged.[67]

In canon 2229, § 3, 3°, it is stated that grave fear does not excuse if the "delict" tends to a contempt of the faith, etc., while in canon 2205, § 3, the Code says that if the "act" tends to such results, the imputability of the delict is not taken away. Some may see herein an indication that the Code wanted to introduce a further distinction, by which canon 2229, § 3, 3°, would be understood to include only those delicts which of their very nature involve such a contempt of the faith, etc., thereby excluding delicts which involve such a contempt or also such harm to souls only by reason of circumstances.[68] However, the authors explicitly state that the act would be imputable in such a case, and imply that there is no such distinction to be made here with reference to *latae sententiae* penalties.[69] This seems the correct interpretation.

[66] *Ius Canonicum,* VII, 215; cf. also Roberti, *De Delictis et Poenis,* I, 278. Claeys Bouuaert *(art. cit., — Jus Pontificium,* VI ([1926], 141) holds that "public" is used here in contradistinction to "private".

[67] Canon 2197, 1°.

[68] As an example the case of a Catholic doctor might be cited, one namely who has been forced by threats to perform an abortion. Ordinarily grave fear would excuse him from the *latae sententiae* penalty. But if the fear were inflicted manifestly in order to make him show contempt of the faith, or of the Church and her teaching, then one who holds this opinion would still excuse him from this same *latae sententiae* penalty of excommunication reserved to the ordinary, (canon 2350, § 1).

[69] Cf. Roberti, *De Delictis et Poenis,* I, 278; Sole, *De Delictis et Poenis,* p. 82.

The use of the different terms "acts" and "delict" is easily explained by the arrangement and import of the different sections of the Code. Canon 2205 speaks of "acts" because it stands in a section of the Code in which human acts are classified as delicts; but canon 2229 uses "delict" because it speaks of penalties and presupposes the existence of delicts. Moreover, if one accepted the above interpretation of "public harm to souls," it would have to be said that there is no *latae sententiae* penalty in the Code wherein fear would not excuse because of public harm to souls. For in none of the crimes among the *latae sententiae* penalties mentioned in the Code as involving harm to souls is this harm of its very nature and necessarily public in the sense of not being occult.[70]

2. Slight Fear in Crimes Wherein Perfect *Dolus* Is Not Postulated

Slight fear does not excuse from *latae sententiae* penalties if the law does not postulate perfect *dolus*. For, as noted above,[71] slight fear does not excuse from imputability in the violation of even a merely ecclesiastical law. And with regard to *latae sententiae* penalties, canon 2229, § 3, 3°, mentions only grave fear. The canon reads: "If the law does not have these terms . . . grave fear does not exempt from *latae sententiae* penalties, if the offense entails contempt . . . " Consequently, if the delict does not entail such contempt or harm, grave fear excuses. But there is no such excuse indicated in any way for slight fear.[72]

III. NECESSITY AND HARDSHIP AS EXCUSES WHEN PERFECT *Dolus* IS NOT POSTULATED

Necessity (grave) and grave hardship by being excusing causes parallel to grave fear in delictual matters[73] must be said to excuse from *latae sententiae* penalties to the same extent that grave fear excuses in those delicts in which either simple *dolus* or *culpa* is sufficient to occasion the incurring of the penalty. These, then, excuse from the *latae sententiae* penalty in all cases wherein the

[70] Cf. *supra,* pp. 97-98.

[71] Cf. *supra,* p. 90. Canon 2205, § 2.

[72] Cf. Crnica, *art. cit.,—Jus Pontificium,* V. (1925), 14.

[73] Cf. canon 2205, § 2.

delict does not imply a contempt of the faith or of ecclesiastical authority, or beget a public harm to souls.

Slight necessity and slight hardship, being parallel to slight fear, do not excuse from *latae sententiae* penalties in those delicts wherein either *dolus* or *culpa* is sufficient.

ARTICLE V. FEAR AS AN EXCUSE FROM *Latae Sententiae* PENALTIES IN THE EXTERNAL FORUM

I. POSSIBLE CONFLICT OF FORUMS

Fear, being essentially internal, may be very difficult or even impossible to prove in the external forum.[74] Consequently, a person may feel quite sure that he did not incur a certain *latae sententiae* penalty due to the presence of grave fear, and yet be unable to produce sufficient evidence to convince a judge or superior in the external forum. And in case the delict is notorious,[75] the observance of the penalty imposed by the law can be demanded in the external forum even without formal court proceedings.[76]

There can be no doubt that an excuse from a *latae sententiae* penalty according to canon 2229 must be admitted in the external forum, provided that the delinquent can prove the presence of such an excusing cause. For the very nature of a declarative sentence, which merely declares that a penalty has been incurred, demands that such causes which have actually excused from the *latae sententiae* penalty be given their merited recognition if their presence can be satisfactorily established by proof. But if the delinquent fails to prove the existence of any of the excusing causes of canon 2229, and the declarative sentence is passed, he must obey it in the external forum, unless the sentence is manifestly unjust for some other reason. This obedience must be demanded for the sake of good order and also for the sake of avoiding all scandal. In the internal forum the delinquent is excused from observing

[74] Cf. *supra*, pp. 106-107.

[75] Canon 2197, 3°.

[76] Canon 2232, § 1.

the penalty, provided that he does not cause scandal through such a non-observance of the penalty.[77]

II. A MITIGATED SENTENCE

Since the excuse of force or fear must be admitted in the external forum when legitimately proved, the judge cannot in such a case declare that the *latae sententiae* penalty enacted by law has been incurred. However, the question does arise whether he can in such an instance impose a milder sentence. The Code itself in paragraph 4 of canon 2229 gives the judge power to impose a mitigated sentence in case of gravely culpable ignorance when the delinquent is excused from the *latae sententiae* censure enacted for a crime which does not postulate perfect *dolus.*[78]

It seems quite certain that the judge cannot impose a mitigated penalty in case one has proved an excuse due to the presence of force or fear. Such a mitigated penalty would have to be expressly provided for in law in order to bring it in compliance with the demands of canon 2195, § 1.[79] In the present penal legislation of the Church there is "no crime, no punishment without previous penal sanctions." [80] And since in penal matters from the viewpoint of the potential delinquent the milder interpretation is to be applied,[81] the existence of this previous penal sanction must be proved. Cappello excludes the possibility of a mitigated sentence in this instance, because canon 2229, § 4, expressly restricts the judge's faculty to the instance of excuse occasioned by gravely culpable ignorance,[82] and in no way extends it to the case of ex-

[77] Cf. Swoboda, *Ignorance,* p. 231; De Meester, *Juris Canonici et Juris Canonico-Civilis Compendium,* (nova ed. 3 vols. in 4, Brugis: Desclée, 1921-1928), III, P. II, 154.

[78] Swoboda *(Ignorance,* p. 232) shows that this does not hold in the case of crimes which postulate perfect *dolus.* He argues that the fact that the Code expressly declares that the judge can impose a mitigated penalty in one case would seem to exclude the other case.

[79] " . . . violatio cui addita sit sanctio canonica saltem indeterminata."

[80] Cf. Michiels, *De Delictis et Poenis,* I, 76-78.

[81] Canon 2219, § 1.

[82] Canon 2229, § 3, 1°.

cuse occasioned by the presence of force or grave fear.[83] This conclusion also conforms to the rule of canon 2228 which demands that a delict be perfectly consummated according to the proper wording of the law. And it is likewise in harmony with pre-Code opinion on this subject.[84]

Lest this opinion seem to injure the usefulness of penal law in maintaining good order, it should be noted that the welfare of society does not demand that every external violation of law be punished, not even every gravely sinful violation.[85] Moreover in case the public good demands it, the judge or superior has an adequate means of imposing a penal remedy. Canon 2222, § 1, seems to allow that if there is a special gravity in the criminal act, despite the influence of force or fear, or if there is grave scandal, the judge by a condemnatory sentence or the superior by a precept can impose a penalty.[86]

It may seem that this is an unwarranted extension of the power of the judge or superior as outlined in canon 2222, § 1, for in this instance here considered the law has a penalty attached, whereas the canon reads, "Even though there is no penalty attached to a law."[87] But it is evidently the sense of the canon that a transgression can be punished if the given scandal or the special gravity of the violation demands it, and the phrase "Even though no penalty is attached" is inserted rather in an extensive than in a restrictive sense. It cannot be objected that this would open the way to a rather broad interpretation of the powers of the judge or superior in these instances. For in every case there must be either a grave scandal or a special gravity in the act itself.

[83] *Art. cit.,—Jus Pontificium,* V (1925), 132. Claeys Bouuaert *(art. cit.,—Jus Pontificium,* VI [1926], 143) thinks the judge would be able to render a mitigated sentence in such a case.

[84] Swoboda *(Ignorance,* p. 232) shows that the opinion that the judge could not impose a lesser penalty in case the delinquent escaped the *latae sententiae* penalty was the common opinion before the Code. He quotes Lega, *Praelectiones In Textum Iuris Canonici—De Delictis et Poenis* (2. ed., Romae, 1910), p. 33.

[85] Cf. Roberti, *art. cit.,—Apollinaris,* XI (1938), 181.

[86] Cf. Swoboda, *Ignorance,* p. 233.

[87] "Licet lex nullam sanctionem appositam habeat, . . . "

A second question in regard to declarative sentences in this connection concerns those circumstances which only partially excuse. Can the judge by a declarative sentence mitigate the *latae sententiae* penalty which is actually incurred, but in which the imputability is diminished, for example, in view of the presence of slight fear in the commission of a delict in which simple *dolus* or *culpa* is sufficient to occasion the incurring of the penalty? The nature of a declarative sentence seems to rule out such a possibility. Since the full penalty is already incurred, the duty of the judge in such a case is merely to declare the fact for the external forum. This was also the common opinion before the Code.[88]

[88] Cf. Lega (1860-1935), *De Delictis et Poenis,* p. 33. He writes: "Ex adverso poenae latae sententiae delictum afficiunt quum fuerit ea ratione consummatum, uti in lege expressum sit. Exinde probabilius est non esse in potestate iudicis huiusmodi poenas minuere per suam sententiam declaratoriam, etsi concurrant causae minuentes. Inquam probabilius est, quia ita opinantur communiter Doctores."

DIAGRAM OF THE INSTANCES OF FEAR AS AN EXCUSE IN REGARD TO *FERENDAE SENTENTIAE* AND TO *LATAE SENTENTIAE* PENALTIES

			FEAR			
			GRAVE		SLIGHT	
			F. S.	*L. S.*	*F. S.*	*L. S.*
PERFECT *DOLUS*	Delicts not intrinsically evil and which do not involve contempt of the faith, etc.		*2205, §§ 2, 3	*2229, § 2	*p. op.	*p. op.
	Delicts intrinsically evil.		*p. op.	*2229, §§ 2, 3, 3°	*p. op.	*p. op.
	Delicts involving contempt of the faith or of ecclesiastical authority.		*p. op.	*p. op.	*p. op.	*p. op.
	Delicts involving harm to souls.	Public	*p. op.	*p. op.	*p. op.	*p. op.
		Occult	*p. op.	*2229, §§ 2, 3, 3°	*p. op.	*p. op.
DOLUS OR *CULPA*	Delicts not intrinsically evil and which do not involve contempt of the faith, etc.		*2205, §§ 2, 3	*2229, § 3, 3°	+	+
	Delicts intrinsically evil.		+2205, § 3	*2229, § 3, 3°	+	+
	Delicts involving contempt of the faith or of ecclesiastical authority.		+2205, § 3	+2229, § 3, 3°	+	+
	Delicts involving harm to souls.	Public	+2205, § 3	+2229, § 3, 3°	+	+
		Occult	+2205, § 3	*2229, § 3, 3°	+	+

In this diagram "*F.S.*" indicates *ferendae sententiae* penalties, while "*L.S.*" indicates *latae sententiae* penalties. The upper diagram refers to delicts in which perfect *dolus* is postulated, while the lower diagram refers to delicts in which either *dolus* or *culpa* is sufficient to render the delinquent responsible for the punishment. "*" indicates that the respective form of fear excuses in the given case; "+" indicates it does not excuse. The numbers indicate corresponding canons of the Code. Cases not clearly solved by these canons are indicated by "p. op." (probable opinion).

CONCLUSIONS

1. Until the time of the Council of Trent few canonists entered upon any separate or thorough consideration of fear as an excuse in criminal acts. Their teaching on fear as an excuse was concerned principally with its effects in contract law.

2. The Scholastics of the 13th century were responsible for introducing into Moral Theology the distinctions of Aristotle regarding the voluntariness of an act committed out of fear. The moral theologians in turn influenced the later canonists who developed the norms which have been substantially received into the Code.

3. Necessity (including grave fear *ab intrinseco)* and grave hardship are to be considered excusing causes parallel to grave fear *(ab extrinseco)* in regard to both imputability and responsibility.

4. Since there is an *involuntarium secundum quid* when an act is performed through slight fear, this fear must be considered as lessening the imputability of the criminal act to some extent. Consequently it excuses when perfect *dolus* is postulated for either a *ferendae sententiae* or a *latae sententiae* penalty. The same is true of slight necessity or slight hardship.

5. Grave or even slight fear which really influences the criminal act excuses from the incurring of *latae sententiae* penalties when perfect *dolus* is postulated, even if the delict tends to a contempt of the faith or of ecclesiastical authority, or involves public harm to souls.

6. When the excuse of force or fear is urged in the external forum, the burden of proof rests always upon the one alleging the force or fear, even if there is question of delicts which postulate perfect *dolus.*

7. The judge or superior cannot impose a mitigated sentence in case the defendant is excused from the *latae sententiae* penalty in view of the force or fear which influenced his act.

8. When a *latae sententiae* penalty is already incurred, the judge cannot by a declarative sentence mitigate the punishment by reason of the diminished imputability which resulted from the presence of fear in the committed delict.

BIBLIOGRAPHY

Sources

Acta Apostolicae Sedis, Commentarium Officiale, Romae, 1909—

Acta Sanctae Sedis, 41 vols., Romae, 1865-1908.

Bullarum Diplomatum et Privilegiorum Sanctorum Romanorum Pontificum Taurinensis Editio, 24 vols. et Appendix, Augustae Taurinorum-Neapoli, 1857-1872.

Canones et Decreta Sacrosancti Oecumenici Concilii Tridentini, Lipsiae, 1866.

Codex Iuris Canonici Pii X Pontificis Maximi iussu digestus Benedicti Papae XV auctoritate promulgatus, Romae: Typis Polyglottis Vaticanis, 1917.

Codicis Iuris Canonici Fontes cura Emi. Petri Card. Gasparri editi., 9 vols., Romae (postea Civitate Vaticana): Typis Polyglottis Vaticanis, 1923-1939. Vols. VII-IX ed. cura et studio Emi. Iustiniani Card. Serédi.

Collectanea S. Congregationis de Propaganda Fide, 2 vols., Romae, ex Typographia Polyglotta Vaticana, 1907.

Corpus Iuris Canonici, ed. Lipsiensis 2. post Aemilii L. Richteri curas instruxit Aemilius Friedberg, Lipsiae: Ex Officina Bernhardi Tauchnitz, 1879-1881. Editio anastatice Repetita, Lipsiae: Tauchnitz, 1928.

Corpus Iuris Civilis, Vol. I, *Institutiones*—recognovit P. Krueger; Vol. II, *Codex Iustinianus—recognovit et retractavit* P. Krueger; Vol. III, *Novellae Constitutiones*—R. Schoell; opus Schoelli morte interceptum absolvit G. Kroll, Berolini: apud Weidmannos, 1928-1929.

————, *Digesta Iustiniani Augusti*—recognoverunt et ediderunt P. Bonfante, C. Fadda, C. Ferrini, S. Riccobono, V. Scialoia, Mediolani: Societá Editrice Libraria, 1931.

Decretum Gratiani Emendatum et Notationibus illustratum una cum glossis, Romae, 1582.

Decretales D. Gregorii Papae IX, una cum glossis restitutae, Romae, 1582.

Hardouin, Jean, *Acta Conciliorum et Epistolae Decretales ac Constitutiones Summorum Pontificum,* 12 vols., Parisiis, 1715.

Jaffé, Philippus, *Regesta Pontificum Romanorum ab condita Ecclesia ad annum post Christum natum MCXCVIII,* 2. ed. cura Wattenbach, Loewenfeld, Kaltenbrunner, Ewald, 2 vols. in 1, Lipsiae: Veit et Comp., 1885-1888.

Liber Sextus Decretalium, una cum Clementinis et Extravagantibus Earumque Glossis Restitutis, Romae, 1582.

Mansi, Joannes, *Sacrorum Conciliorum Nova et Amplissima Collectio,* 53 vols. in 60, Parisiis, Arnemii, Lipsiae, 1901-1927.

Potthast, Augustus, *Regesta Pontificum Romanorum inde ab anno Post Christum Natum MCXCVIII ad annum MCCCIV,* 2 vols., Berolini, 1874-1875.

Quinque Compilationes Antiquae, ed. Aemilius Friedberg, Lipsiae, 1882.

S. Romanae Rotae Decisiones seu Sententiae (ab anno 1909), Romae, Typis Vaticanis, 1912—

Reference Works

Aichner, Simon, *Compendium Iuris Ecclesiastici,* 9. ed., Brixnae, 1900.

Alexander Hales, *Summa Theologiae,* ed. PP. Collegii S. Bonaventurae, 3 vols., Ad Claras Aquas: Typographia Collegii S. Bonaventurae, 1924-1930.

Alphonsus Liguori, St., *Theologia Moralis,* ed. L. Gaudé, 4 vols., Romae, Typis Polyglottis Vaticanis, 1905-1912.

Aristotle, *Basic Works of,* ed. Richard McKeon, Random House, New York, 1941.

Ayrinhac, H. A., and Lydon, P. J., *Penal Legislation in the New Code of Canon Law,* revised edition, New York: Benziger, 1936.

[Bachofen], Charles Augustine, *A Commentary on the New Code of Canon Law,* 8 vols., Vol. VIII, *Penal Code,* St. Louis: Herder, 1922.

Ballerini, Antonius, et Palmieri, Dominicus, *Opus Theologicum Morale,* 7 vols., Prati, 1889-1893.

Barbosa, Augustinus, *Collectanea Doctorum tum Veterum quam Recentorum in Jus Pontificium Universum,* 5 vols., Lugduni, 1637.

Bernardus Papiensis, *Summa Decretalium,* ed. Laspeyres, Ratisbonae, 1860.

Berutti, Christophorus, *Institutiones Iuris Canonici,* Vol. VI, *De Delictis et Poenis,* Taurini-Romae: Marietti, 1938.

Beste, Udalricus, *Introductio in Codicem,* Collegeville, Minn.; St. John's Abbey Press, 1938.

Blat, Albertus, *Commentarium Textus Codicis Iuris Canonici,* 5 vols. in 6, Romae, 1921-1927; Liber V, *De Delictis et Poenis,* Romae, Collegio Angelico, 1924.

Bonaventura, St., *Opera Omnia,* ed. PP. Collegii S. Bonaventurae, 8 vols., Ad Claras Aquas: Typographia Collegii S. Bonaventurae, 1892-1898.

Bouquillon, Thomas, *Theologia Moralis Fundamentalis,* 2. ed., Brugis, 1890.

Bouscaren, T. Lincoln, *The Canon Law Digest,* 2 vols., Milwaukee: The Bruce Publishing Co., 1934-1943.

Cajetan, Thomas, *Commentaria ad Doctoris Angelici Opera Omnia iussu impensaque Leonis XIII, P. M.* edita, Romae, 1882—; IIa IIae, Romae, 1897.

Cappello, Felix, *De Censuris iuxta Codicem Iuris Canonici,* Taurinorum Augustae: Marietti, 1919.

Carr, Thomas J., *The Constitution "Apostolicae Sedis Moderationi" Explained,* Dublin, 1879.

Cavigioli, Ioannes, *De Censuris Latae Sententiae quae in Codice Juris Canonici Continentur Commentariolum,* Torino, 1918.

Cerato, Prosdocimus, *Censurae Vigentes Ipso Facto a Codice Iuris Canonici Excerptae,* 2. ed., Patavii: Typis Seminarii, 1921.

Chelodi, Ioannes, *Jus Poenale et Ordo Procedendi in Iudiciis Criminalibus,* Tridenti: Libr. Edit. Tridentum, 1920, reprinted, 1925.

Cicognani, Hamletus, *Canon Law,* authorized English version, by J. O'Hara and F. Brennan, Philadelphia: Dolphin Press, 1935.

Cipollini, Albertus, *De Censuris Latae Sententiae iuxta Codicem Iuris Canonici,* Taurini, Marietti, 1925.

Cocchi, Guidus, *Commentarium in Codicem Iuris Canonici,* 5 vols. in 8, 1922-1930. Liber V, *De Delictis et Poenis,* Taurinorum Augustae: Marietti, 1925.

Coronata, Mathaeus, Conte a, *Institutiones Iuris Canonici,* 5 vols.; Vols. I-II, 2. ed., 1939; Vols. III-V, 1933-1936, Taurini: Marietti.

Corpus Iuris, ed. Mack and Hale, New York, American Law Book Co., 1918.

Covarrubias y Leyva, Didacus, *Opera Omnia,* 2 vols., Coloniae Allobrogum, 1679.

Croce, Isidorus, *Textus Selecti ex operibus Commentatorum Byzantinorum Iuris Ecclesiastici.* Fonti, Serie II—Fascicolo V, Civitate Vaticana: Typis Polyglottis Vaticanis, 1939.

D'Annibale, Josephus, *In Constitutionem Apostolicae Sedis Commentarii,* 5. ed., Romae, 1909.

————, *Summula Theologiae Moralis,* 5. ed., 3 vols., Romae, 1908.

De Brabandere, et A. De Meester, *Iuris Canonici Compendium,* 8. ed., Brugis, 1914-1916.

De Meester, Alphonsus, *Juris Canonici et Juris Canonici-Civilis Compendium,* nova ed., 3 vols. in 4, Brugis: Descleé, 1921-1928.

Doheny, William J., *Canonical Procedure in Matrimonial Cases,* Milwaukee: Bruce, 1938.

Eichmann, Edward, *Lehrbuch des Kirchenrechts auf Grund des Codex Iuris Canonici,* 2. ed., Paderborn, Schöningh, 1926.

————, *Das Strafrecht des Codex Iuris Canonici,* Paderborn: Schöningh, 1920.

Fagnanus, Prosper, *Commentaria in Quinque Libros Decretalium,* 4 vols., Romae, 1661.

Ferraris, Lucius, *Bibliotheca Canonica Iuridica Moralis Theologica nec non Ascetica Polemica Rubricistica Historica,* 9 vols., Romae, 1885-1899.

Ferrini, Contardo, *Diritto Penale Romano, Teorie Generali,* Milano, 1899.

Gury, Ioannes, et Ballerini, Antonius, *Compendium Theologiae Moralis,* 3. ed., 2 vols., Romae, 1874-1875.

Harper, *Latin Dictionary,* ed. Lewis and Short, Oxford: Clarendon Press, 1882.

Hinschius, Paul, *Das Kirchenrecht der Katholiken und Protestanten in Deutschland,* 6 vols., Berlin, 1869 1897.

Hollweck, Joseph, *Die kirchlichen Strafgesetze,* Mainz, 1899.

Hostiensis, Cardinalis (Henricus de Segusio), *Commentaria in Quinque Decretalium Libros,* 5 vols. in 3, Venetiis, 1581.

————, *Summa Aurea,* Lugduni, 1568.

Huser, Roger J., *The Crime of Abortion in Canon Law,* The Catholic University of America Canon Law Studies, n. 162, Washington, D. C.: The Catholic University of America Press, 1942.

Ioannes Andeae, *In Sex Decretalium Libros Novella Commentaria,* 6 vols. in 5, Venetiis, 1581.

Konings, Antonius, *Theologia Moralis,* 4. ed., 2 vols., New York, 1880.

Kuttner, Stephan, *Kanonistische Schuldlehre von Gratian bis auf die Dekretalen Gregors IX,* Studi e Testi, n. 64, Città del Vaticano: Biblioteca Apostolica Vaticana, 1935.

Latini, Ioseph, *Iuris Criminalis Philosophici Summa Lineamenta,* Romae: Marietti, 1924.

Laymann, Paulus, *Theologia Moralis,* Venetiis, 1719.

Leech, George L., *A Comparative Study of the Constitution "Apostolicae Sedis" and the "Codex Iuris Canonici."* The Catholic University of America Canon Law Studies, n. 15, Washington, D. C.: The Catholic University of America, 1922.

Lega, Michael, *Praelectiones in Textum Iuris Canonici—De Delictis et Poenis,* 2. ed., Romae, 1910.

Lehmkuhl, Augustinus, *Theologia Moralis,* 5. ed., 2 vols., Friburgi Brisgoviae, 1888.

Maroto, Philippus, *Institutiones Iuris Canonici,* 2 vols., Romae: Apud Commentarium pro Religiosis, 1919.

Merkelbach, Benedictus H., *Summa Theologiae Moralis,* 3 vols., Vols. I-II, 3. ed., 1938; Vol. III, 3. ed., 1939, Parisiis: Desclee.

Michael, Jerome, and Wechsler, Herbert, *Criminal Law and Its Administration,* Chicago: The Foundation Press, 1940.

Michiels, Gommarus, *Normae Generales Juris Canonici,* 2 vols., Lublin: Universitas Catholica, 1929.

———, *De Delictis et Poenis,* Vol. I, *De Delictis,* Lublin, Universitas Catholica, 1934.

Migne, Jacques P., *Patrologiae Cursus Completus,* Series Latina, 221 vols., Parisiis, 1858-1864.

Mocchegiani, P., *Iurisprudentia Ecclesiastica ad Usum et Commoditatem Utriusque Cleri,* 3 vols., Quaracchi, 1905.

Moersdorf, Klaus, *Die Rechtssprache des Codex Juris Canonici,* Paderborn: Schöningh, 1937.

Mommsen, Theodore, *Le Droit Pénal Romain,* trans. by J. Duquesne, 3 vols., Paris, 1907.

Moriarity, Eugene J., *Oaths in Ecclesiastical Courts,* The Catholic University of America Canon Law Studies, n. 110, Washington, D. C.: The Catholic University of America, 1937.

Moriarity, Francis, *The Extraordinary Absolution from Censures,* The Catholic University of America Canon Law Studies, n. 113, Washington, D. C.: The Catholic University of America, 1938.

Noldin, H., et Schmitt, A., *Summa Theologiae Moralis,* 3 vols., Vol. I, 23. ed., 1935; Vol. II, 22. ed., 1934; Vol. III, 23. ed., 1935, Oeniponte: Rauch.

Noldon, H., et Schönegger, A., *De Censuris,* 28. ed., Oeniponte: Rauch, 1935

Noval, Josephus, *Commentarium Codicis Iuris Canonici,* Lib. IV, *De Processibus,* Pars I, *De Iudiciis,* Augustae Taurinorum: Marietti, 1920.

Ojetti, Benedictus, *Synopsis Rerum Moralium et Iuris Pontificii,* 3. ed., 4 vols., Romae, 1909-1914.

Panormitanus, Abbas (Nicolaus de Tudeschis), *Commentarium in Quinque Libros Decretalium,* 5 vols. in 7, Venetiis, 1588.

Passerinus, Petrus, *Commentaria in Sextum Librum Decretalium,* Venetiis, 1698.

Pighi, J. B., *Censurae Sententiae Latae et Irregularitates,* 7. ed., Veronae: Sorores Cinquetti Filiae Felicis, 1922.

Pirhing, Ernricus, *Jus Canonicum in Libros Decretalium,* 5 vols., Dilingae, 1722.

Plöchl, Willibald, *Das Eherecht des Magisters Gratianus,* Wiener Staats-und-Rechtswissenschaftliche Studien, n. 24, Leipzig, Wien: Franz Deutike, 1935.

Raymundus a Penyafort, St., *Summa iuris canonici,* Veronae, 1744.

Roberti, Franciscus, *De Delictis et Poenis,* Vol. I, editio altera, Romae: Libraria Pontificii Instituti Utriusque Iuris, 1938.

Rufinus, *Summa Decretorum,* ed. Singer, Paderborn, 1902.

Salmanticenses, *Cursus Theologicus Summam D. Thomae Complectens,* 20 vols., Parisiis, Bruxellis, 1871-1885.

Sanchez, *De Sancto Matrimonii Sacramento,* 3 vols. in 2, Antverpiae, 1607.

————, *Opus Morale in Praecepta Decalogi,* Parmae, 1723.

Sandaeus, Felinus, *Commentaria in Quinque Libros Decretalium,* 2 vols., Venetiis, 1570.

Sangmeister, Joseph V., *Force and Fear as Precluding Matrimonial Consent,* The Catholic University of America Canon Law Studies, n. 80, Washington, D. C.: The Catholic University of America, 1932.

Santi, Franciscus, et Leitner, Martin, *Praelectiones Iuris Canonici,* 4. ed., 5 vols. in 2, Ratisbonae, 1903-1905.

Sayre, F. Bowes, *A Selection of Cases on Criminal Law,* Rochester, N. Y.: The Lawyers Co-Operative Publishing Company, 1927.

Schmalzgrueber, Franciscus, *Jus Ecclesiasticum Universum,* 5 vols. in 12, Romae, 1843-1845.

Scotus, John Duns, *Opera Omnia,* 26 vols., Parisiis, 1891-1895.

Sipos, Stephanus, *Enchiridion Iuris Canonici,* 2. ed., Pécs: "Haladas R.T.", 1931.

Smith, S. B., *Elements of Ecclesiastical Law,* Vol. III, *Ecclesiastical Punishments,* 3. ed., New York, 1888.

————, *The New Procedure in Criminal and Disciplinary Causes of Ecclesiastics in the United States,* New York, 1887.

Sole, Jacobus, *De Delictis et Poenis,* Romae: Pustet, 1920.

Sporer, Patricius, *Theologia Moralis Decalogalis et Sacramentalis,* ed. I. Bierbaum, 3 vols., Paderbornae, 1897-1901.

Suarez, Franciscus, *Opera Omnia,* 26 vols., Parisiis, 1856-1866.

————, *Summa,* 2 vols., Parisiis, 1858.

Swoboda, I, *Ignorance in Relation to the Imputability of Delicts,* The Catholic University of America Canon Law Studies, n. 143, Washington, D. C.: The Catholic University of America Press, 1941.

Thomas Aquinas, St., *Opera Omnia,* 16 vols., Venetiis, 1595.

————, *Doctoris Angelici Opera Omnia iussu impendaque Leonis XIII, P.M.* edita, Romae, 1882—; IIa IIae, Romae, 1897.

————, *Summa Theologica,* Impensis Studii Generalis, O. Pr. Ottawa, Canada, 1942.

Toso, Albertus, *Ad Codicem Iuris Canonici Commentaria Minora,* Vol. I, Taurini, Romae: Marietti, 1921.

Van Hove, A., *Commentarium Lovaniense in Codicem Iuris Canonici,* Vol. I, Tom. II, *De Legibus Ecclesiasticis,* Mechliniae: H. Dessain, 1930.

Vermeersch, A.-Creusen, J., *Epitome Iuris Canonici,* Vol. I, 6. ed., 1937; Vols. II-III, 5. ed., 1934-1936, Mechliniae: H. Dessain.

Wernz, Franciscus, *Ius Decretalium,* 6 vols., Romae et Prati, 1906-1913.

Wernz, Franciscus, et Vidal, Petrus, *Ius Canonicum,* 7 vols. in 8, Romae: Universitas Gregoriana, 1923-1938.

Woywod, Stanislaus, *A Practical Commentary on the Code of Canon Law,* 5. ed., 2 vols., New York, Jos. F. Wagner, 1939.

Articles

Bieter, F. E., "The Canon Law on Deceit"—*ER,* LXVI (1922), 42-51.

Bruehl, Charles, "Fear and Guilt"—*HPR* XXVI (1925-1926), 1-8.

Cappello, Felix, "Tres Quaestiones Circa Censuras"—*Jus Pontificium,* V (1925), 124-132.

Claeys Bouuaert, F., "De metus influxu quoad valorem actuum et quoad delicta et poenas secundum Codicem Juris Cononici"—*Jus Pontificium,* VI (1926), 105-111; 138-144.

Crnica, Antonius, "De metu gravi ut causa eximente a poenis latae sententiae" —*Jus Pontificium,* V (1925), 9-15.

Glaser, Joseph, "Pastoral-Fälle"—*LQS,* LXXXIII (1930), 120-125.

Hall, Livingston, and Seligman, Selig J., "Mistake of Law and Mens Rea"—*University of Chicago Law Review,* VIII (June 1941), 641-682.

Oesterle, G., "Ex Privata Jurisprudentia"—*Jus Pontificium,* X (1930), 250.

Roberti, Franciscus, "De Metu Indirecto quoad Negotia Iuridica praesertim Matrimonium"—*Apollinaris,* XI (1938), 557-561.

Vermeersch, Arthurus, "De Metu qui, saltem ex lege positiva, excusat ab obligationibus vitiato consensu susceptis, praecipue de metu ab intrinseco vel extrinseco"—*Periodica,* XVII (1928), 138*-144*.

PERIODICALS

Apollinaris, Romae, 1928—

American Ecclesiastical Review, The (formerly *The Ecclesiastical Review*), Philadelphia, 1889-1943; Baltimore, 1944—

Homiletic and Pastoral Review, The, New York, 1900—

Jus Pontificium, Romae, 1921—

Periodica de Re Canonica et Morali Utili praesertim Religiosis et Missionariis, Brugis, 1905-1927;

———, *de Re Morali, Canonica, Liturgica,* Brugis, 1928-1936; Romae, 1937—

Theologisch-praktische Quartalschrift, Linz, 1832—

University of Chicago Law Review, The, Chicago, 1933—

Zeitschrift der Savigny-Stiftung für Rechtsgeschichte, Roman, Abtlg., Weimar, 1880—

———, *Kanon, Abtlg.,* Weimar, 1911—

ABBREVIATIONS

AAS—*Acta Apostolicae Sedis.*
ASS—*Acta Sanctae Sedis.*
C.—Codex (Justinianus).
D.-Digestum (Justinianum).
ER—*Ecclesiastical Review.*
Fontes—*Codicis Iuris Canonici Fontes.*
HPR—*Homiletic and Pastoral Review.*
Jaffé—*Regesta Pontificum Romanorum.*
JE—Jaffé-Ewald.
JK—Jaffé-Kaltenbrunner.
JL—Jaffé-Loewenfeld.
LQS—*Theologisch-praktische Quartalschrift* (Linz).
N.—Novellae (Justinianae).
Periodica—*Periodica de Re Canonica et Morali.*
Potthast—*Regesta Pontificum Romanorum.*
S.R.R. Dec.—*S.R. Rotae Decisiones seu Sententiae.*

ALPHABETICAL INDEX

BIOGRAPHICAL NOTE

Alan Edward McCoy was born at Spokane, Washington, October 7, 1913. He attended the parochial schools of St. Aloysius, and of St. Francis of Assisi at Spokane, Washington. In June, 1932, he graduated from St. Anthony's College, Santa Barbara, California; entered the Novitiate of the Franciscan Order at San Luis Rey, California, and in the following year made his religious profession as a member of the Franciscan Order. After completing his philosophical studies at the Old Mission, San Luis Rey, California, he made his theological studies at the Old Mission, Santa Barbara, California. He was ordained to the priesthood at the Old Mission, Santa Barbara, California, June 12, 1938. In September, 1941 he entered the School of Canon Law at the Catholic University of America, where he received the Baccalaureate in Canon Law in May, 1942, and the Licentiate in Canon Law in May, 1943.

CANON LAW STUDIES *

1. FRERIKS, REV. CELESTINE A., C.PP.S., J.C.D., Religious Congregations in Their External Relations, 121 pp., 1916.
2. GALLIHER, REV. DANIEL M., O.P., J.C.D., Canonical Elections, 117 pp., 1917.
3. BORKOWSKI, REV. AURELIUS L., O.F.M., J.C.D., De Confraternitatibus Ecclesiasticis, 136 pp., 1918.
4. CASTILLO, REV. CAYO, J.C.D., Disertacion Historico-Canonica sobre la Potestad del Cabildo en Sede Vacante o Impedida del Vicario Capitular, 99 pp., 1919 (1918).
5. KUBELBECK, REV. WILLIAM J., S.T.B., J.C.D., The Sacred Penitentiaria and Its Relation to Faculties of Ordinaries and Priests, 129 pp., 1918.
6. PETROVITS, REV. JOSEPH, J.C., S.T.D., J.C.D., The New Church Law on Matrimony, X-461 pp., 1919.
7. HICKEY, REV. JOHN J., S.T.B., J.C.D., Irregularities and Simple Impediments in the New Code of Canon Law, 100 pp., 1920.
8. KLEKOTKA, REV. PETER J., S.T.B., J.C.D., Diocesan Consultors, 179 pp. 1920.
9. WANENMACHER, REV. FRANCIS, J.C.D., The Evidence in Ecclesiastical Procedure Affecting the Marriage Bond, 1920 (Printed 1935).
10. GOLDEN, REV. HENRY FRANCIS, J.C.D., Parochial Benefices in the New Code, IV-119 pp., 1921 (Printed 1925).
11. KOUDELKA, REV. CHARLES J., J.C.D., Pastors, Their Rights and Duties According to the New Code of Canon Law, 211 pp., 1921.
12. MELO, REV. ANTONIUS, O.F.M., J.C.D., De Exemptione Regularium, X-188 pp., 1921.
13. SCHAAF, REV. VALENTINE THEODORE, O.F.M., S.T.B., J.C.D., The Cloister, X-180 pp., 1921.
14. BURKE, REV. THOMAS JOSEPH, S.T.D., J.C.D., Competence in Ecclesiastical Tribunals, IV-117 pp., 1922.
15. LEECH, REV. GEORGE LEO, J.C.D., A Comparative Study of the Constitution "Apostolicae Sedis" and the "Codex Juris Canonici," 179 pp., 1922.
16. MOTRY, REV. HUBERT LOUIS, S.T.D., J.C.D., Diocesan Faculties According to the Code of Canon Law, II-167 pp. 1922.
17. MURPHY, REV. GEORGE LAWRENCE, J.C.D., Delinquencies and Penalties in the Administration and the Reception of the Sacraments, IV-121 pp., 1923.
18. O'REILLY, REV. JOHN ANTHONY, S.T.B., J.C.D., Ecclesiastical Sepulture in the New Code of Canon Law, II-129 pp., 1923.

* Below n. 100 only the following numbers are still available: No. 3, 4, 9, 25, 34 57 and 75. Beginning with n. 100 only the following are unavailable: Nn. 100-111 inclusive, and n. 113.

19. Michalicka, Rev. Wenceslas Cyrill, O.S.B., J.C.D., Judicial Procedure in Dismissal of Clerical Exempt Religious, 107 pp., 1923.
20. Dargin, Rev. Edward Vincent, S.T.B., J.C.D., Reserved Cases According to the Code of Canon Law, IV-103 pp., 1924.
21. Godfrey, Rev. John A., S.T.B., J.C.D., The Right of Patronage According to the Code of Canon Law, 153 pp., 1924.
22. Hagedorn, Rev. Francis Edward, J.C.D., General Legislation on Indulgences, II-154 pp., 1924.
23. King, Rev. James Ignatius, J.C.D., The Administration of the Sacraments to Dying Non-Catholics, V-141 pp., 1924.
24. Winslow, Rev. Francis Joseph, O.F.M., J.C.D., Vicars and Prefects Apostolic, IV-149 pp., 1924.
25. Correa, Rev. Jose Servelion, S.T.L., J.C.D., La Potestad Legislativa de la Iglesia Catolica, IV-127 pp., 1925.
26. Dugan, Rev. Henry Francis, A.M., J.C.D., The Judiciary Department of the Diocesan Curia, 87 pp., 1925.
27. Keller, Rev. Charles Frederick, S.T.B., J.C.D., Mass Stipends, 167 pp., 1925.
28. Paschang, Rev. John Linus, J.C.D., The Sacramentals According to the Code of Canon Law, 129 pp., 1925.
29. Piontek, Rev. Cyrillus, O.F.M., S.T.B., J.C.D., De Indulto Exclaustrationis necnon Saecularizationis, XIII-289 pp., 1925.
30. Kearney, Rev. Richard Joseph, S.T.B., J.C.D., Sponsors at Baptism According to the Code of Canon Law, IV-127 pp., 1925.
31. Bartlett, Rev. Chester Joseph, A.M., LL.B., J.C.D., The Tenure of Parochial Property in the United States of America, V-108 pp., 1926.
32. Kilker, Rev. Adrian Jerome, J.C.D., Extreme Unction, V-425 pp., 1926.
33. McCormick, Rev. Robert Emmett, J.C.D., Confessors of Religious, VIII-266 pp., 1926.
34. Miller, Rev. Newton Thomas, J.C.D., Founded Masses According to The Code of Canon Law, VII-93 pp., 1926.
35. Roelker, Rev. Edward G., S.T.D., J.C.D., Principles of Privilege According to the Code of Canon Law, XI-166 pp., 1926.
36. Bakalarczyk, Rev. Richardus, M.I.C., J.U.D., De Novitiatu, VIII-208 pp., 1927.
37. Pizzuti, Rev. Lawrence, O.F.M., J.U.L., De Parochis Religiosis, 1927. (Not Printed.)
38. Bliley, Rev. Nicholas Martin, O.S.B., J.C.D., Altars According to the Code of Canon Law, XIX-132 pp., 1927.
39. Brown, Mr. Brendan Francis, A.B., LL.M., J.U.D., The Canonical Juristic Personality with Special Reference to Its Status in the United States of America, V-212 pp., 1927.
40. Cavanaugh, Rev. William Thomas, C.P., J.U.D., The Reservation of the Blessed Sacrament, VIII-101 pp., 1927.

41. DOHENY, REV. WILLIAM J., C.S.C., A.B., J.U.D., Church Property: Modes of Acquisition, X-118 pp.. 1927.
42. FELDHAUS, REV. ALOYSIUS H., C.PP.C., J.C.D., Oratories, IX-141 pp., 1927.
43. KELLY, REV. JAMES PATRICK, A.B., J.C.D., The Jurisdiction of the Simple Confessor, X-208 pp., 1927.
44. NEUBERGER, REV. NICHOLAS J., J.C.D., Canon 6 or the Relation of the Codex Juris Canonici to the Preceding Legislation, V-95 pp., 1927.
45. O'KEEFE, REV. GERALD MICHAEL, J.C.D., Matrimonial Dispensations, Powers of Bishops, Priests, and Confessors, VIII-232 pp., 1927.
46. QUIGLEY, REV. JOSEPH A. M., A.B., J.C.D., Condemned Societies, 139 pp., 1927.
47. ZAPLOTNIK, REV. JOHANNES LEO, J.C.D., De Vicariis Foraneis, X-142 pp., 1927.
48. DUSKIE, REV. JOHN ALOYSIUS, A.B., J.C.D., The Canonical Status of the Orientals in the United States, VIII-196 pp., 1928.
49. HYLAND, REV. FRANCIS EDWARD, J.C.D., Excommunication, Its Nature, Historical Development and Effects, VIII-181 pp., 1928.
50. REINMANN, REV. GERALD JOSEPH, O.M.C., J.C.D., The Third Order Secular of Saint Francis, 201 pp., 1928.
51. SCHENK, REV. FRANCIS J., J.C.D., The Matrimonial Impediments of Mixed Religion and Disparity of Cult, XVI-318 pp., 1929.
52. COADY, REV. JOHN JOSEPH, S.T.D., J.U.D., A.M., The Appointment of Pastors, VIII-150 pp., 1929.
53. KAY, REV. THOMAS HENRY, J.C.D., Competence in Matrimonial Procedure, VIII-164 pp., 1929.
54. TURNER, REV. SIDNEY JOSEPH, C.P., J.U.D., The Vow of Poverty, XLIX-217 pp., 1929.
55. KEARNEY, REV. RAYMOND A., A.B., S.T.D., J.C.D., The Principles of Delegation, VII-149 pp., 1929.
56. CONRAN, REV. EDWARD JAMES, A.B., J.C.D., The Interdict, V-163 pp., 1930.
57. O'NEILL, REV. WILLIAM H., J.C.D., Papal Rescripts of Favor, VII-218 pp., 1930.
58. BASTNAGEL, REV. CLEMENT VINCENT, J.U.D., The Appointment of Parochial Adjutants and Assistants, XV-257 pp., 1930.
59. FERRY, REV. WILLIAM A., A.B., J.C.D., Stole Fees, V-136 pp., 1930.
60. COSTELLO, REV. JOHN MICHAEL, A.B., J.C.D., Domicile and Quasi-Domicile, VII-201 pp., 1930.
61. KREMER, REV. MICHAEL NICHOLAS, A.B., S.T.B., J.C.D., Church Support in the United States, VI-136 pp., 1930.
62. ANGULO, REV. LUIS, C.M., J.C.D., Legislation de la Iglesia sobre la intencion en la application de la Santa Misa, VII 104 pp., 1931.
63. FREY, REV. WOLFGANG NORBERT, O.S.B., A.B., J.C.D., The Act of Religious Profession, VIII-174 pp., 1931.

64. ROBERTS, REV. JAMES BRENDAN, A.B., J.C.D., The Banns of Marriage, XIV-140 pp., 1931.
65. RYDER, REV. RAYMOND ALOYSIUS, A.B., J.C.D., Simony, IX-151 pp., 1931.
66. CAMPAGNA, REV. ANGELO, PH.D., J.U.D., Il Vicario Generale del Vescovo, VII-205 pp., 1931.
67. COX, REV. JOSEPH GODFREY, A.B., J.C.D., The Administration of Seminaries, VI-124 pp., 1931.
68. GREGORY, REV. DONALD J., J.U.D., The Pauline Privilege, XV-165 pp., 1931.
69. DONOHUE, REV. JOHN F., J.C.D., The Impediment of Crime, VII-110 pp., 1931.
70. DOOLEY, REV. EUGENE A., O.M.I., J.C.D., Church Law on Sacred Relics, IX-143 pp., 1931.
71. ORTH, REV. CLEMENT RAYMOND, O.M.C., J.C.D., The Approbation of Religious Institutes, 171 pp., 1931.
72. PERNICONE, REV. JOSEPH M., A.B., J.C.D., The Ecclesiastical Prohibition of Books, XII-267 pp., 1932.
73. CLINTON, REV. CONNELL, A.B., J.C.D., The Paschal Precept, IX-108 pp., 1932.
74. DONNELLY, REV. FRANCIS B., A.M., S.T.L., J.C.D., The Diocesan Synod, VIII-125 pp., 1932.
75. TORRENTE, REV. CAMILO, C.M.F., J.C.D., Las Processiones Sagradas, V-145 pp., 1932.
76. MURPHY, REV. EDWIN J., C.PP.S., J.C.D., Suspension Ex Informata Conscienta, XI-122 pp., 1932.
77. MACKENZIE, REV. ERIC F., A.M., S.T.L., J.C.D., The Delict of Heresy in its Commission, Penalization, Absolution, VII-124 pp., 1932.
78. LYONS, REV. AVITUS E., S.T.B., J.C.D., The Collegiate Tribunal of First Instance, XI-147 pp., 1932.
79. CONNOLLY, REV. THOMAS A., J.C.D., Appeals, XI-195 pp., 1932.
80. SANGMEISTER, REV. JOSEPH V., A.B., J.C.D., Force and Fear as Precluding Matrimonial Consent, V-211 pp., 1932.
81. JAEGER, REV. LEO A., A.B., J.C.D., The Administration of Vacant and Quasi-Vacant Episcopal Sees in the United States, IX-229 pp., 1932.
82. RIMLINGER, REV. HERBERT T., J.C.D., Error Invalidating Matrimonial Consent, VII-79 pp., 1932.
83. BARRETT, REV. JOHN D. M., S.S., J.C.D., A Comparative Study of the Third Plenary Council of Baltimore and the Code, IX-221 pp., 1932.
84. CARBERRY, REV. JOHN J., PH.D., S.T.D., J.C.D., The Juridical Form of Marriage, X-177 pp., 1934.
85. DOLAN, REV. JOHN L., A.B., J.C.D., The Defensor Vinculi, XII-157 pp., 1934.
86. HANNAN, REV. JEROME D., A.M., S.T.D., LL.B., J.C.D., The Canon Law of Wills, IX-517 pp., 1934.

87. LEMIEUX, REV. DELISE A., A.M., J.C.D., The Sentence in Ecclesiastical Procedure, IX-131 pp., 1934.
88. O'ROURKE, REV. JAMES J., A.B., J.C.D., Parish Registers, VII-109 pp., 1934.
89. TIMLIN, REV. BARTHOLOMEW, O.F.M., A.M., J.C.D., Conditional Matrimonial Consent, X-381 pp., 1934.
90. WAHL, REV. FRANCIS X., A.B., J.C.D., The Matrimonial Impediments of Consanguinity and Affinity, VI-125 pp., 1934.
91. WHITE, REV. ROBERT J., A.B., LL.B., S.T.B., J.C.D., Canonical Ante-Nuptial Promises and the Civil Law, VI-152 pp., 1934.
92. HERRERA, REV. ANTONIO PARRA, O.C.D., J.C.D., Legislacion Ecclesiastica sobra el Ayuno y Abstinencia, XI-191 pp., 1935.
93. KENNEDY, REV. EDWIN J., J.C.D., The Special Matrimonial Process in Cases of Evident Nullity, X-165 pp., 1935.
94. MANNING, REV. JOHN J., A.B., J.C.D., Presumption of Law in Matrimonial Procedure, XI-111 pp., 1935.
95. MOEDER, REV. JOHN M., J.C.D., The Proper Bishop for Ordination and Dimissorial Letters, VII-135 pp., 1935.
96. O'MARA, REV. WILLIAM A., A.B., J.C.D., Canonical Causes for Matrimonial Dispensations, IX-155 pp., 1935.
97. REILLY, REV. PETER, J.C.D., Residence of Pastors, IX-81 pp., 1935.
98. SMITH, REV. MARINER T., O.P., S.T.Lr., J.C.D., The Penal Law for Religious, VIII-169 pp., 1935.
99. WHALEN, REV. DONALD W., A.M., J.C.D., The Value of Testimonial Evidence in Matrimonial Procedure, XIII-297 pp., 1935.
100. CLEARY, REV. JOSEPH F., J.C.D., Canonical Limitations on the Alienation of Church Property, VIII-141 pp., 1936.
101. GLYNN, REV. JOHN C., J.C.D., The Promoter of Justice, XX-337 pp., 1936.
102. BRENNAN, REV. JAMES H., S.S., M.A., S.T.B., J.C.D., The Simple Convalidation of Marriage, VI-135 pp., 1937.
103. BRUNINI, REV. JOSEPH BERNARD, J.C.D., The Clerical Obligations of Canons 139 and 142, X-121 pp., 1937.
104. CONNOR, REV. MAURICE, A.B., J.C.D., The Administrative Removal of Pastors, VIII-159 pp., 1937.
105. GUILFOYLE, REV. MERLIN JOSEPH, J.C.D., Custom, XI-144 pp., 1937.
106. HUGHES, REV. JAMES AUSTIN, A.B., A.M., J.C.D., Witnesses in Criminal Trials of Clerics, IX-140 pp., 1937.
107. JANSEN, REV. RAYMOND J., A.B., S.T.L., J.C.D., Canonical Provisions for Catechetical Instruction, VII-153 pp., 1937.
108. KEALY, REV. JOHN JAMES, A.B., J.C.D., The Introductory Libellus in Church Court Procedure, XI-121 pp., 1937.
109. MCMANUS, REV. JAMES EDWARD, C.SS.R., J.C.D., The Administration of Temporal Goods in Religious Institutes, XVI-196 pp., 1937.

110. Moriarty, Rev. Eugene James, J.C.D., Oaths in Ecclesiastical Courts, X-115 pp., 1937.
111. Rainier, Rev. Eligius George, C.SS.R., J.C.D., Suspension of Clerics, XVII-249 pp., 1937.
112. Reilly, Rev. Thomas F., C.SS.R., J.C.D., Visitation of Religious, VI-195 pp., 1938.
113. Moriarty, Rev. Francis E., C.SS.R., J.C.D., The Extraordinary Absolution from Censures, XV-334 pp., 1938.
114. Connolly, Rev. Nicholas P., J.C.D., The Canonical Erection of Parishes, X-132 pp., 1938.
115. Donovan, Rev. Jamess Joseph, J.C.D., The Pastor's Obligation in Prenuptial Investigation, XII-322 pp., 1938.
116. Harrigan, Rev. Robert J., M.A., S.T.B., J.C.D., The Radical Sanation of Invalid Marriages, VIII-208 pp., 1938.
117. Boffa, Rev. Conrad Humbert, J.C.D., Canonical Provisions for Catholic Schools, VII-211 pp., 1939.
118. Parsons, Rev. Anscar John, O.M.Cap., J.C.D., Canonical Elections, XII-236 pp., 1939.
119. Reilly, Rev. Edward Michael, A.B., J.C.D., The General Norms of Dispensation, XII-156 pp., 1939.
120. Ryan, Rev. Gerald Aloysius, A.B., J.C.D., Principles of Episcopal Jurisdiction, XII-172 pp., 1939.
121. Burton, Rev. Francis James, C.S.C., A.B., J.C.D., A Commentary on Canon 1125, X-222 pp., 1940.
122. Miaskiewicz, Rev. Francis Sigismund, J.C.D., Supplied Jurisdiction According to Canon 209, XII-340 pp., 1940.
123. Rice, Rev. Patrick William, A.B., J.C.D., Proof of Death in Prenuptial Investigation, VIII-156 pp., 1940.
124. Anglin, Rev. Thomas Francis, M.S., J.C.D., The Eucharistic Fast, VIII-183 pp., 1941.
125. Coleman, Rev. John Jerome, J.C.D., The Minister of Confirmation, VI-153 pp., 1941.
126. Downs, Rev. Joseph Emmanuel, A.B., J.C.D., The Concept of Clerical Immunity, XI-163 pp., 1941.
127. Esswein, Rev. Anthony Albert, J.C.D., Extrajudicial Penal Powers of Ecclesiastical Superiors, X-144 pp., 1941.
128. Farrell, Rev. Benjamin Francis, M.A., S.T.L., J.C.D., The Rights and Duties of the Local Ordinary Regarding Congregations of Women Religious of Pontifical Approval, V-195 pp., 1941.
129. Feeney, Rev. Thomas John, A.B., S.T.L., J.C.D., Restitutio in Integrum, VI-169 pp., 1941.
130. Findlay, Rev. Stephen William, O.S.B., A.B., J.C.D., Canonical Norms Governing the Deposition and Degradation of Clerics, XVII-279 pp., 1941.

131. Goodwine, Rev. John, A.B., S.T.L., J.C.D., The Right of the Church to Acquire Property, VIII-119 pp., 1941.
132. Heston, Rev. Edward Louis, C.S.C., Ph.D., S.T.D., J.C.D., The Alienation of Church Property in the United States, XII-222 pp., 1941.
133. Hogan, Rev. James John, A.B., S.T.L., J.C.D., Judicial Advocates and Procurators, XIII-200 pp., 1941.
134. Kealy, Rev. Thomas M., A.B., Litt.B., J.C.D., Dowry of Women Religious, IX-152 pp., 1941.
135. Keene, Rev. Michael James, O.S.B., J.C.D., Religious Ordinaries and Canon 198, V-164 pp., 1942.
136. Kerin, Rev. Charles A., SS., M.A., S.T.B., J.C.D., The Privation of Christian Burial, XVI-279 pp., 1941.
137. Louis, Rev. William Francis, M.A., J.C.D., Diocesan Archives, X-101 pp., 1941.
138. McDevitt, Rev. Gilbert Joseph, A.B., J.C.D., Legitimacy and Legitimation, X-247 pp., 1941.
139. McDonough, Rev. Thomas Joseph, A.B., J.C.D., Apostolic Administrators, X-217 pp., 1941.
140. Meier, Rev. Carl Anthony, A.B., J.C.D., Penal Administrative Procedure Against Negligent Pastors, XI-240 pp., 1941.
141. Schmidt, Rev. John Rogg, A.B., J.C.D., The Principles of Authentic Interpretation in Canon 17 of the Code of Canon Law, XII-331 pp., 1941.
142. Slafkosky, Rev. Andrew Leonard, A.B., J.C.D., The Canonical Episcopal Visitation of the Diocese, X-197 pp., 1941.
143. Swoboda, Rev. Innocent Robert, O.F.M., J.C.D., Ignorance in Relation to the Imputability of Delicts, IX-271 pp., 1941.
144. Dube, Rev. Arthur Joseph, A.B., J.C.D., The General Principles for the Reckoning of Time in Canon Law, VIII-299 pp., 1941.
145. McBride, Rev. James T., A.B., J.C.D., Incardination and Excardination of Seculars, XX-585 pp., 1941.
146. Krol, Rev. John T., J.C.D., The Defendant in Ecclesiastical Trials, XII-207 pp., 1942.
147. Comyns, Rev. Joseph J., C.SS.R., A.B., J.C.D., Papal and Episcopal Administration of Church Property, XIV-155 pp., 1942.
148. Barry, Rev. Garrett Francis, O.M.I., J.C.D., Violation of the Cloister, XII-260 pp., 1942.
149. Bolduc, Rev. Gatien, C.S.V., A.B., S.T.L., J.C.D., Les Études dans les Religions Cléricales, VIII-155 pp., 1942.
150. Boyle, Rev. David John, M.A., J.C.D., The Juridic Effects of Moral Certitude on Pre-Nuptial Guarantees, XII-188 pp., 1942.
151. Canavan, Rev. Walter Joseph, M.A., Litt.D., J.C.D., The Profession of Faith, XII-143 pp., 1942.
152. Desrochers, Rev. Bruno, A.B., Ph.L., S.T.B., J.C.D., Le Premier Concile Plénier de Québec et le Code de Droit Canonique, XIV-186 pp., 1942.

153. Dillon, Rev. Robert Edward, A.B., J.C.D., Common Law Marriage, X-148 pp., 1942.
154. Dodwell, Rev. Edward John, Ph.D., S.T.B., J.C.D., The Time and Place for the Celebration of Marriage, X-156 pp., 1942.
155. Donnellan, Rev. Thomas Andrew, A.B., J.C.D., The Obligation of the Missa pro Populo, VII-131 pp., 1942.
156. Eltz, Rev. Louis Anthony, A.B., J.C.L., Cooperation in Crime.
157. Gass, Rev. Sylvester Francis, M.A., J.C.D., Ecclesiastical Pensions, XI-206 pp., 1942.
158. Guiniven, Rev. John Joseph, C.SS.R., J.C.D., The Precept of Hearing Mass, XIV-188 pp., 1942.
159. Gulczynski, Rev. John Theophilus, J.C.D., The Desecration and Violation of Churches, X-126 pp., 1942.
160. Hammill, Rev. John Leo, M.A., J.C.D., The Obligations of the Traveler According to Canon 14, VIII-204 pp., 1942.
161. Haydt, Rev. John Joseph, A.B., J.C.D., Reserved Benefices, XI-148 pp., 1942.
162. Huser, Rev. Roger John, O.F.M., A.B., J.C.D., The Crime of Abortion in Canon Law, XII-187 pp., 1942.
163. Kearney, Rev. Francis Patrick, A.B., S.T.L., J.C.L., The Principles of Canon 1127.
164. Linahen, Rev. Leo James, S.T.L., J.C.D., De Absolutione Complicis in Peccato Turpi, 114 pp., 1942.
165. McCloskey, Rev. Joseph Aloysius, A.B., J.C.D., The Subject of Ecclesiastical Law According to Canon 12, XVII-246 pp., 1942.
166. O'Neill, Rev. Francis Joseph, C.SS.R., J.C.D., The Dismissal of Religious in Temporary Vows, XIII-220 pp., 1942.
167. Prince, Rev. Joseph Edward, A.B., S.T.B., J.C.D., The Diocesan Chancellor, X-136 pp., 1942.
168. Riesner, Rev. Albert Joseph, C.SS.R., J.C.D., Apostates and Fugitives from Religious Institutes, IX-168 pp., 1942.
169 Stenger, Rev. Joseph Bernard, J.C.D., The Mortgaging of Church Property, 186 pp., 1942.
170. Waldron, Rev. Joseph Francis, A.B., J.C.D., The Minister of Baptism, XII-197 pp., 1942.
171. Willett, Rev. Robert Albert, J.C.D., The Probative Value of Documents in Ecclesiastical Trials, X-124 pp., 1942.
172. Woeber, Rev. Edward Martin, M.A., J.C.D., The Interpellations, XII-161 pp., 1942.
173. Benko, Rev. Matthew Aloysius, O.S.B., M.A., J.C.L., The Abbott *Nullius*.
174. Christ, Rev. Joseph James, M.A., S.T.L., J.C.L., Dispensation from Vindicative Penalties.
175. Clancy, Rev. Patrick M. J., O.P., A.B., S.T.Lr., J.C.D., The Local Religious Superior, X-229 pp., 1943.

176. CLARKE, REV. THOMAS JAMES, J.C.D., Parish Societies, XII-147 pp., 1943.
177. CONNOLLY, REV. JOHN PATRICK, S.T.L., J.C.D., Synodal Examiners and Parish Priest Consultors, X-223 pp., 1943.
178. DRUMM, REV. WILLIAM MARTIN, A.B., J.C.L., Hospital Chaplains.
179. FLANAGAN, REV. BERNARD JOSEPH, A.B., S.T.L., J.C.D., The Canonical Erection of Religious Houses, X-147 pp., 1943.
180. KELLEHER, REV. STEPHEN JOSEPH, A.B., S.T.B., J.C.D., Discussions with Non-Catholics: Canonical Legislation, X-93 pp., 1943.
181. LEWIS, REV. GORDIAN, C.P., J.C.D., Chapters in Religious Institutes, XII-169 pp., 1943.
182. MARX, REV. ADOLPH, J.C.D., The Declaration of Nullity of Marriages Contracted Outside the Church, X-151 pp., 1943.
183. MATULENAS, REV. RAYMOND ANTHONY, O.S.B., A.B., J.C.L., Communication, a Source of Privileges.
184. O'LEARY, REV. CHARLES GERARD, C.SS.R., Religious Dismissed After Perpetual Profession.
185. POWER, REV. CORNELIUS MICHAEL, J.C.L., The Blessing of Cemeteries.
186. SHUHLER, REV. RALPH VINCENT, O.S.A., J.C.D., Privileges of Religious to Absolve and Dispense, XII-195 pp., 1943.
187. ZIOLKOWSKI, REV. THADDEUS STANISLAUS, A.B., J.C.D., The Consecration and Blessing of Churches, XII-151 pp., 1943.
188. HENEGHAN, REV. JOHN JOSEPH, S.T.D., J.C.L., The Marriages of Unworthy Catholics: Canons 1065 and 1066.
189. CARROLL, REV. COLEMAN FRANCIS, M.A., S.T.L., J.C.L., Charitable Institutions.
190. CIESLUK, REV. JOSEPH EDWARD, Ph.B., S.T.L., J.C.L., National Parishes in the United States.
191. COBURN, REV. VINCENT PAUL, A.B., J.C.L., Marriages of Conscience.
192. CONNORS, REV. CHARLES PAUL, C.S.Sp., A.B., J.C.L., Extra-Judicial Procurators in the Code of Canon Law.
193. COYLE, REV. PAUL RAYMOND, A.B., J.C.L., Judicial Exceptions.
194. FAIR, REV. BARTHOLOMEW FRANCIS, A.B., S.T.L., J.C.L., The Impediment of Abduction.
195. GALLAGHER, REV. THOMAS RAPHAEL, O.P., A.B., S.T.Lr., J.C.L., The Examination of the Qualities of the Ordinand.
196. GANNON, REV. JOHN MARK, S.T.L., J.C.L., The Interstices Required for the Promotion of Orders.
197. GOLDSMITH, REV. J. WILLIAM, B.C.S., S.T.L., J.C.L., The Competence of Church and State Over Marriage—Disputed Points.
198. GOODWINE, REV. JOSEPH GERARD, A.B., S.T.B., J.C.L., The Reception of Converts.
199. KOWALSKI, REV. ROMUALD EUGENE, O.F.M., A.B., J.C.L., Sustenance of Religious Houses of Regulars.

200. McCoy, Rev. Alan Edward, O.F.M., J.C.L., Force and Fear in Relation to Delictual Imputability and Penal Responsibility.
201. McDevitt, Rev. Vincent John, Ph.B., S.T.L., J.C.L., Perjury.
202. Martin, Rev. Thomas Owen, Ph.D., S.T.D., J.C.L., Adverse Possession, Prescription and Limitation of Actions: The Canonical "Praescriptio."
203. Miklosovic, Rev. Paul John, A.B., J.C.L., Attempted Marriages and Their Consequent Juridic Effects.
204. Mundy, Rev. Thomas Maurice, A.B., S.T.L., J.C.L., The Union of Parishes.
205. O'Dea, Rev. John Coyle, A.B., J.C.L., The Matrimonial Impediment of Nonage.
206. Olalia, Rev. Alexander Ayson, S.T.L., J.C.L., A Comparative Study of the Christian Constitution of States and the Constitution of the Philippine Commonwealth.
207. Poisson, Rev. Pierre-Marie, C.S.C., A.B., Ph.L., Th.L., J.C.L., Droits Patrimoniaux des Maisons et des Eglises Religieuses.
208. Stadalnikas, Rev. Casimir Joseph, M.I.C., J.C.L., Reservation of Censures.
209. Sullivan, Rev. Eugene Henry, S.T.L., J.C.L., Proof of the Reception of the Sacraments.
210. Vaughan, Rev. William Edward, J.C.L., Constitutions for Diocesan Courts.
211. Lyons, Rev. Joseph Henry, J.C.L., The Joinder of Issue in Canonical Trials.

www.ingramcontent.com/pod-product-compliance
Lightning Source LLC
LaVergne TN
LVHW050226080826
844660LV00012B/482
* 9 7 8 0 8 1 3 2 2 3 8 7 2 *